Bigger Than Yourself

Bigger Than Yourself

SHORT DISCUSSIONS ON
MORE ABUNDANT LIVING

BY WENDELL J. ASHTON

BOOKCRAFT
Salt Lake City, Utah

LITHOGRAPHED IN U.S.A.
BY

PUBLISHERS PRESS

SALT LAKE CITY, UTAH

Dedicated to
Owen
and
Kay

Contents

BOOK ONE—GLADNESS IN MY HEART   *Page*

Tallest Living Things 19
Just an Optimist............................ 22
A Woman, Too?............................ 26
Westport.................................. 29
Ten Words for Today........................ 32
No Finer Gift.............................. 35
Glow and Grow............................ 39
Sweet Togetherness......................... 42
Timing................................... 45

BOOK TWO—FULLNESS OF JOY

Counsel from a Cow........................ 51
Warrior's Wisdom.......................... 54
Power in a Pencil.......................... 57
Secret of His Wisdom....................... 60
Sugar.................................... 63
Keep the Freckles!......................... 66
Two Streets in One........................ 69
He Did His Homework...................... 72
Birds in the Bush.......................... 76

BOOK THREE—ENLARGE MY STEPS

Time for Greatness......................... 81
Youthful Maturity.......................... 84
When a Boy Becomes a Man................. 87
They Made Other Kings..................... 90
If We Want to Win......................... 93
Top Dog.................................. 96
Give Yourself a Spur....................... 99
"He Held His Spear".......................102
Lions Among Men..........................105

BOOK FOUR—RESTORETH MY SOUL

Wings for Your Hopes......................111
End of the World..........................114
Maginot Lines............................117
Dumping Slag.............................120

Page

What's Next?" 123
Christmas Tree Country 127
With Wings or on Foot 130
By the Golden Gate 133
Hero Where He Lost 136

BOOK FIVE—BE OF GOOD COURAGE

David's Finest Hour 141
Rebel in London 144
Second Chance 148
Ride to Freedom 151
Ultimatums 154
Try! 157
Stan the Man 160
Boulder in the Stream .163
Man With a Doctrine 166

BOOK SIX—MAKE ME TO HEAR JOY

What Kind of Egg 173
Let Us Reason Together 176
With No Crutches 179
Strangler Fig 182
Margin of Mastery 185
They Think Tall 188
Problems or Challenges? 191
When the Alps Are Bitter Cold 194
"Go-Givers" 197

BOOK SEVEN—ENTER WITH THANKSGIVING

Summit of Life 203
Tender Heart 206
Whistler's Mother 209
To Be Appreciated 212
Master in Giving 215
Thanksgiving 218
Mother of Fifteen 221
The Art of Praise 224
Adventure Next Door .230

Preface

Every man (and woman too) is much bigger than he himself realizes.

That is the lesson which continues to recur as one catches glimpses of greatness in the lives of others. Through the ages wise men have spoken and written of that lesson. With words that have become scripture, prophets have told of it too. None has lifted that lesson to the heights where Jesus Himself placed it.

This little volume attempts to reflect some of the messages of that lesson as the author has caught them from others.

This collection of observations is actually a continuation of two previous ones by the author: *It's Your Life to Enjoy,* originally published by Bookcraft in 1955, and *In Your Own Image,* appearing in 1959. All are taken primarily from the author's articles published monthly on the back cover of *The Instructor.*

The volume is divided into seven chapters, each introduced by a brief verse from that ancient book of soul stirring lyrics: *Psalms.* The approximate date when each article was written appears on the front page of each.

First of all, the author is grateful to those whose lives and words these messages attempt to reflect. Appreciation also goes to Kenneth S. Bennion for his monthly suggestions and helps. Lorin F. Wheelwright, chairman of *The Instructor* committee, and Boyd O. Hatch, the magazine's managing editor, and their associates have also helped considerably.

The author expresses gratitude to Marvin W. Wallin of Bookcraft for his continuing friendship, encouragement, and many courtesies. The index was prepared by Paul R. Green, who also assisted considerably with the format.

If this humble volume helps the reader to realize in some measure the greatness that is within him, the author will be grateful.

— Wendell J. Ashton

BOOK ONE

Gladness in My Heart

"Thou hast put gladness in my heart   .   .   ."
—Psalm 4:7

TALLEST LIVING THINGS

MY FIRST JOB FOR PAY WAS IN A lumber yard. My father was the manager, and to keep me out of summer mischief he put me to work.

It did not take me long to discover that few things were so miserable to handle as bundles of cedar shingles. They filled my arms with tiny, itching slivers. Oak flooring was tough, too. It seemed hard as steel and almost as heavy. Big slivers came from pine and fir.

But one type of lumber I early learned to like was redwood. It was smooth as satin. Redwood was deep-red in color, like raspberry sherbet, and was light in weight. Even in the hand of a 10-year-old, a saw would cut easily through redwood. Redwood's even texture took paint well. And its rich, natural color stained beautifully. Redwood glued well, resisted rot, termites, fire, and rust. Redwood had good insulation properties.

When our first little frame home was built, we made sure its exterior walls were covered with redwood shakes.

It therefore was with more than ordinary interest that we caught our first glimpse of the giant redwoods of northern California. They stand impressively tall,

———————

April, 1964

like pillars reaching towards the heavens. The purplish-red bark is thick and deep fluted. Often the stately columns reach upwards one hundred feet before their feathery foliage appears — almost as delicate as a green forest haze.

Some of these forest patriarchs began pushing toward the sun even before Jesus was born in Bethlehem.

But what was most impressive about the redwoods was their height. We learned that one of them is three hundred fifty-nine feet high. They are the tallest living things on earth.

In this particular grove, we learned that redwoods often grow in groups. We saw families of them standing as if in council. Here were charred stumps and living trees with deep scars from fires, the most recent between one hundred fifty and two hundred years ago. From the roots of giants felled or wounded by flames, sprouts have emerged. Now there are circles of lofty monarchs.

The highest living things often grow tall in groups. So do men.

Laura Z. Hobson, an International News Service writer, some years ago described a flood which hit Dublin. Six dray horses were caught in a stable. As water began filling the stable, the animals were released and swam to high ground. When the last horse arrived, a crowd noticed mice jump off his back.

This incident reminded Laura Hobson of something a native of Dublin had written. He was George Bernard Shaw. He had written repeatedly in his plays and books that the surest way to find happiness is to give yourself over to a cause bigger than yourself.

There are some great causes in the world. But the

basic cause for every man is his own family. That is what the redwoods seem to say. That is what the prophets have said. Yes, a man grows taller when he grows with his family.

A family makes a man bigger than himself. The Prince of Peace no doubt could have entered the world alone. But he came into a family. He repeatedly reminded men, too, that the family continues far beyond this brief earthly span. He spoke of His Heavenly Father who had sent Him.[1] On earth He prayed to that Father.[2] He said He would return to His Father.[3]

Yes, a man's family continues longer than the centuries-old circles of the redwoods. A man's family can extend into eternity. A man is exalted through his family.

A man's earthly stature reaches higher, too, as he feels the "pull" of a kingly kinsman, even as a redwood sprout pushes upward alongside a sky-piercing elder. It is only natural, too, for a man to grow taller when he sees taller — when he realizes his footprints extend into eternity as against earthly time. A man grows tall when he measures life and men in the framework of timeless tomorrows as against a day, a year, a decade, or even a century.

These are thoughts which can stir you in the sylvan quietude, stir you as you stand before a circle of redwoods, the tallest living things.

---

[1] See *John* 20-21.
[2] See *Matthew* 26:39.
[3] See *John* 20:17.

JUST AN OPTIMIST

His eyes beamed as he answered my questions. We sat on a big, dark-green, leather sofa in the hotel lobby.

"The future looks extremely bright," he said. There was a toughness in his broad, tanned face. His silver hair was thinning and receding; but he continued to talk spiritedly, like a boy on Christmas Eve. "We expect a ten per cent gain in our potato volume next year," he added. "Our fertilizer production should be up 25 to 30 per cent."

After our brief chat, I related our conversation to another businessman in the hotel lobby. "Oh, he is just an optimist," my acquaintance said.

Yes, the man is an optimist; but his record is impressive. He [1] is one of the nation's large processors of potatoes. His company is now turning out thirty different potato items, from frozen French fries to hashbrowns. And the records show that America's per capita consumption of processed potatoes has risen from less than two pounds in 1940 to nearly 36 pounds in 1962. [2]

The more we look about us, the more we see optimists

_____

December, 1963
[1] J. R. Simplot of Boise, Idaho.
[2] *Wall Street Journal,* Aug. 13, 1963.

pushing the world toward new, exciting horizons. Conrad Nicholson Hilton, who directs a 293-million-dollar around-the-world hotel chain, is described in a *Time* [3] cover article as an "eternal optimist." The magazine illustrates the point with a word picture of the 75-year-old hotelman sitting on the terrace of his 61-room mansion in Bel Air, California. He was about to take off on a world-circling trip. He sat with a handful of peanuts, and he whistled loudly again and again for a half-domesticated bluejay which flew away months before. Conrad Hilton refused to give up hope that his feathered friend will one day return.

Some of the great optimists are often those who may not appear to be such.

We find no mention in the New Testament that Jesus laughed or even smiled. But the record does tells us that He wept over the death of Lazarus. In the synagogue, He was grieved because of the hardness of the Pharisees' hearts. Again, as they came seeking a sign, ". . . He sighed deeply in his spirit." [4] In Gethsemane He was ". . . sorrowful and very heavy." [5]

But as we follow in the footsteps of Jesus, we realize that He was the supreme Optimist. He told the poor in spirit that theirs would be the kingdom of heaven. He assured those who prayed to the Father in secret that He would reward them openly.

The humble Nazarene said that he who seeks shall find, and ". . . to him that knocketh it shall be opened." [6]

---

[3] *Time*, July 19, 1963, pages 63-72.
[4] *Mark* 8:12.
[5] *Matthew* 26:37.
[6] *Matthew* 7:8.

To the centurion whose servant was stricken with palsy, the Master gave assurance that he would be healed. To a man beside a pool in Bethesda, infirm for 38 years, He said: ". . . Rise, take up thy bed, and walk." [7]

Repeatedly to His Twelve He said that He would rise on the third day after His death. To the Eleven, after the Last Supper, He said, looking to the future: "In my Father's house are many mansions. . . . I go to prepare a place for you." [8]

Hanging painfully on the cross, He assured the nearby malefactor that they would be together that very day in paradise.

The world had never seen optimism like that.

To Peter, near Bethany, Jesus said: ". . . What things soever ye desire, when ye pray, believe that ye receive them, and ye shall have them." [9] On another occasion he said that a man with the faith of a mustard seed could move mountains.

Jesus said that through Him, men would live again. All will receive a resurrection as did He. To some, He said, even godhood lies ahead.

Those are the promises of the Master, the Optimist who told the sick man to arise and walk. And he did. Those are the assurances of Him who said he would rise on the third day. And he did.

The optimism of Jesus brought new hope to the world. No wonder at His birth the wise men ". . . rejoiced with exceeding great joy." [10] No wonder the

---

[7] *John* 5:8.
[8] *John* 14:2.
[9] *Mark* 11:24.
[10] *Matthew* 2:10.

angel said to the shepherds watching their flocks by night: ". . . I bring you good tidings of great joy. . . ." [11]

Perhaps he did not realize what a compliment he was really paying, when that businessman said of another in the hotel lobby: "Oh, he is just an optimist."

---

[11] *Luke* 2:10.

A WOMAN, TOO?

When Jesus was born in Bethlehem, He was visited by shepherds, the scriptures say. The shepherds had learned of His birth from an angel while watching their flocks at night. They found the infant Messiah in a manger, with His mother and Joseph.

The records also describe a visit to the Christ Child in Bethlehem by wise men from the East. They fell down and worshipped Him and presented Him with gifts of gold, frankincense, and myrrh.

But I have been wondering tonight if, while the Babe was in Bethlehem, He was not visited by a woman. The scriptures do not say. But there must have been a woman who helped Joseph minister to Mary — helped bathe the Babe, provide Him clean clothes, and prepare meals for His mother.

There must have been a woman at the manger, a woman like our neighbor who left this life the other day. We all called her Donna.[1] I remember her at Christmas time a year ago. Weak and wan, her slender form rose in our chapel. Donna was up briefly from an agonizing sickbed of many days. Her hazel-blue eyes smiled as she spoke of her love for Jesus. "I feel His nearness," she said. "Through him I find hope and

_____

December, 1962
[1] Donna Boyack (Mrs. B. R.) Greenwood.

take heart. I know that He is my Redeemer. I know that He lives."

We were stirred. We were strengthened.

On New Year's Day, Donna, a mother of four, arose from her sickbed and called at each of her neighbors. "Just wanted to wish you a happy New Year," she began. "I appreciate you as a neighbor and all you do for me and my family."

But Donna often went far beyond the front door in her kindnesses to others. After she had gone, I was shown a letter she received a few weeks before. The penmanship was labored. The note was from an elderly woman in Phoenix, Arizona, who had lived temporarily with neighbors of Donna. In part, the letter read:

"When I was down sick, you took care of me, got my check cashed, took care of my money, went down the street, got my medicine, and got the elders of your Church to pray over me. . . . Dear Donna, you are like a mother to me."

Donna's eldest son, class president at his university, told me of a middle-of-the-night experience shortly before his mother passed away with cancer. He had a cold and was coughing. As he continued, he heard someone stumbling to his bedside. It could not be his mother. She had not been up from her sickbed for three weeks. But it was. "What can I do for you?" she whispered.

At dawn of her final earthly day, her husband called me to join him at her bedside. She was too weak to speak. But as we prepared to administer to her, her thin hand stroked our arms. Silently her fingers intoned her deep appreciation.

Pinned to the drapery near her bed was a verse:

    Lord, make me an instrument of Thy Peace:
    Where there is hatred, let me sow love;
    Where there is injury, pardon;
    Where there is doubt, faith;
    Where there is despair, hope;
    Where there is darkness, light;
    Where there is sadness, joy;
    O Divine Master, grant that I may not so much seek
        to be consoled as to console;
    To be understood as to understand;
    To be loved as to love;
    For it is in giving that we receive,
    It is in pardoning we are pardoned,
    And it is in dying that we are born to eternal life.[2]

Our neighborhood has its Donnas. Other neighborhoods have theirs. No doubt there were Donnas in Bethlehem that holy night when the angels heralded the birth of Jesus. The shepherds were doubtless good men. So were the wise men. And good men usually are so, in large measure, because of good women. There must have been a woman visit Jesus in the manger. There must have been a woman there, a woman like Donna.

---

[2] Author: Saint Francis of Assisi.

WESTPORT

YESTERDAY I DISCOVERED WESTPORT, and I never expect to experience another town quite like it.

Westport is on Washington's coast, about a three-hour drive southwest of Seattle. Downtown Westport is a cluster of brightly painted little frame buildings hugging the edge of a narrow strip of timbered land which pokes into the Pacific like a beckoning finger.

At 6 a.m. Westport is cheerfully awake, like a tree full of robins. Happy people move in and out of the town's dozen or so restaurants. Others talk expectantly in the small shops, trimmed in sky blue, canary yellow, coral, chartreuse or other youthful shades. Men and women wear heavy mackinaws or worn coats, denim, and rubber soled shoes.

Everywhere you see Westport's slogan: "Salmon Capital of the World." That is a big line for a town of only a thousand or so people. But Westport people are different.

I learned that fact shortly before 7 a.m. yesterday when I went aboard the 40-foot yellow and brown fishing boat, *Holiday*. There we were greeted by the skipper's helper, Jerry Pratt. Jerry had keen hazel

_____

September, 1962

twenty-nine

eyes, flashing under heavy brows and dark, crew cut hair.

Jerry was a high school senior. Yet he admitted working on the boat for eight years. He bubbled with spirited anticipation as we moved out to sea.

"Just let out about 20 to 30 feet of line," the skipper called. Eleven of us held poles.

There was little action. Then, after about an hour, our teen-age daughter Susan began tugging at her pole. Moving over the deck like a cat, Jerry was soon at her side. "Give your pole a quick upward jerk," he said.

Susan kept winding her reel. Soon the water below her was churning. Jerry stood ready with his gaffing pole. In a flash, he stabbed the squirming fish and lifted it aboard. It looked as though it would weigh about eight pounds.

"Sea bass," Jerry said matter-of-factly.

"Good meat, that bass," the skipper added. "Kind they use where you buy fish and chips."

"But why didn't Jerry use the more sure landing net instead of a gaff on the bass?" we wondered.

We soon got the idea. A sea bass was something mediocre. It did not really seem to count with Jerry. He was fishing for the king. Only the king, or its smaller brother, the silver salmon, seemed to count with Jerry.

"In other places they call this biggest of salmon the chinook, the tyee, or the spring," the skipper explained. "Here we call it the king."

To Jerry the king was the monarch of game fish all right. This was the fighter. This was the salmon which would leap up waterfalls ten feet high, or rapids even higher, on its way upstream to spawn. This was the real black-backed beauty, usually from five to fifty pounds of sheer spunk.

Jerry was fishing for the king.

It was what you would call a rather skimpy day of fishing. But when a king hit, Jerry was ablaze with excitement.

As the day wore on, I hooked on to my first and only fish. It was a small halibut. Jerry obligingly unhooked it and put it in the boat locker. I had enjoyed baked halibut for dinner. I had seen fishermen elsewhere exult over a halibut. But not Jerry.

He was after the king.

Our fishing came to an end about 3 p.m. We had about an hour's journey back to the harbor.

"How many fish have we caught altogether?" someone called to Jerry.

"Five," he answered.

Then we counted. There were two big sea bass, my halibut, four silvers and a ten-pound king. But Jerry had counted only the salmon.

He fished for the king.

Next morning we paused at the docks. As fishermen walked down the ramps to the boats, Jerry came along.

"Going out today?" he called.

"Afraid not," I replied.

And that was the last we saw of him — walking jauntily toward the boats, head high and chatting happily with a companion. Perhaps there was a reason the whole town of Westport seemed to be like him: youthfully vibrant, though the town was over a hundred years old. All Westport seemed to do as did he.

They fished for the king.

TEN WORDS FOR TODAY

IT WAS SPRINGTIME. JESUS HAD BEEN teaching a vast multitude. There were five thousand men, besides women and children. They had lingered, and He had fed them with the loaves and fishes as they sat on the grass.

The Master directed His Twelve to depart by boat. As they rowed toward the other side of Galilee, He dismissed the throng. Then He found a secluded place on a hill. As darkness fell, He began to pray.

Meanwhile, a storm had arisen on the sea. A head wind ripped into the apostles' boat. Then angry waves began to maul the little craft.

Out in the storm the apostles saw their Master walking on the waters toward them. They were terror-stricken, thinking Him a spirit. In anguish they cried out.

Then the Prince of Peace called: ". . . Be of good cheer; it is I; be not afraid." [1]

Tonight, starting with the events which have been called the first Easter, I have been scanning back across His earthly ministry. It is full of messages of comfort and hope for these heaving times. But none is for today more than that call in the storm to His worried associates.

———————

April, 1962
[1] *Matthew* 14:27; also *Mark* 6:50.

Every man today needs to realize more than ever that to meet growing tensions of the times, to enjoy success in face of stiffening competition, to help others more effectively, he must always strive to *be of good cheer*.

Jesus, earlier in His ministry, had commanded the bedridden man with palsy to ". . . be of good cheer; . . ." [2] Again, shortly before His betrayal, He said to His apostles: ". . . In the world ye shall have tribulations; but be of good cheer; . . ." [3]

There is a blond man, deaf and speechless, who polishes the brass on the entrance of our office building. Whenever I catch his glance he answers with a cheerful grunt and smiling eyes. Then there is a nearby farm youth who has become a world champion fighter. [4] In the midst of a bruising title battle, he can turn between rounds and wink to his wife. I think of Lincoln losing his spirited battle with Douglas for a seat in the Senate. The tall backwoods attorney quipped in defeat that he felt like the boy who stubbed his toe: "It hurt too bad to laugh, and he was too big to cry."

"Be of good cheer," Jesus said in the storm.

His words, "It is I," were reassuring. They call for faith — faith to realize that He is always near. In His final words to those same apostles, as recorded by Matthew, He said: ". . . I am with you alway, even unto the end of the world. . ." [5] Today I heard a neighbor, a woman battling cancer, brighten her friends with her words affirming His nearness.

---

[2] *Matthew* 9:2.
[3] *John* 16:33.
[4] Gene Fullmer.
[5] *Matthew* 28:20.

He remains near now as in the storm on Galilee.

Jesus on the sea also called for courage: "Be not afraid."

Dwight D. Eisenhower, while President, was asked by a reporter how it felt to handle "the toughest job in the world." He answered that it was frustrating but held heartening experiences. Then he told of a visit by 18-year-old Sandra Miskelly of Keane, New Hampshire. An attack of polio two years before had kept her from a visit to the President. In her determination to walk again, he said, she had broken both legs. While recovering she kept up with her school work by telephone. She had been graduated as valedictorian.[6]

In the storm, Jesus called for courage.

Moses had commanded the people not to kill. Jesus asked men not to be angry with another. The older law taught love of kinsmen. Jesus counseled all men to love their enemies. Moses gave Ten Commandments. On Galilee that stormy night Jesus gave ten words — words for today:

"Be of good cheer; it is I; be not afraid."

---

[6] Associated Press, in Los Angeles *Times*, June 3, 1954.

NO FINER GIFT

THE CLOUDS HAD BEEN HANGING
heavy over my head for some three weeks. My doctor
had given me a real scare. Each night I had gone to
bed wondering whether I would ever wake up again.

Then on this particular winter morning I awoke
singing a tune I could not remember hearing for months
or even years. Besides, I was never known to carry a
tune, let alone do solo. But the words burst out:

"Oh, what a beautiful mornin'
Oh, what a beautiful day.
I've got a wonderful feelin'.
Everything's goin' my way!"

The words kept ringing through my head all day long.
Things started getting better. They were soon back
to normal.

I later learned that those lines came from a man who
frequently said: "I just can't write anything without
hope in it." He is the late Oscar Hammerstein II, and
the words are from *Oklahoma!* Hammerstein wrote the
lyrics; his collaborator, Richard Rodgers, the melody.
That hope-giving theatrical hit appeared during one of
the world's darkest hours, in the midst of World War
II.

———————

December, 1960

Yes, I had seen and heard *Oklahoma!* I had felt the pull of its lines about a fresh, beautiful morn with "a bright golden haze on the meadow."

Associates said Oscar Hammerstein was a healing sort of fellow. People in trouble liked to lean on his huge, warm frame. And he liked to lean on a tall captain's table. There, standing up for hours that grew into days, he wrote words that brought new hope to a battered world. In *Carousel,* he wrote: "When you walk through a storm, hold your head up high, . . . and you'll never walk alone." Into *The King and I* he put: "On a bright cloud of music shall we fly?"

As I look back across the years, among the brightest gifts to me have been messages of hope, like Hammerstein's. There was a big, bald former football hero called "Pug." [1] He used to enter our dressing room after we had been trampled in basketball. "Keep fighting," he would say. "You'll get them one of these years." His was a great gift — of giving hope. There was a churchman-author [2] who took time from a heavy load to give me hope as a stumbling, bumbling young writer. An aunt's letters kept me as a boy wanting to reach upward.

No one has given out so much hope, though, as He who gave to men everywhere their first Christmas. On the night of His birth, a message of hope came from the heavens to the shepherds: ". . . for, behold, I bring you good tidings of great joy, which shall be to all people." [3]

---

[1] Homer C. Warner
[2] John A. Widtsoe
[3] *Luke* 2:10.

The Babe in Bethlehem years later Himself gave hope to a little one. When Jesus was asked who was greatest in heaven, He called for a small child.

To a trembling big fisherman named Peter, describing himself as a sinner, He said: ".   .   .   Fear not; from henceforth thou shalt catch men." [4] He stood up against the accusers of a woman taken in sin, and said: ".   .   .   Neither do I condemn thee: go, and sin no more." [5]

Jesus gave hope to a humble child. He gave hope, too, to the sinner whom men would condemn.

To Martha of Bethany, mourning the death of her brother, Lazarus, He consoled: ".   .   .   Thy brother shall rise again." [6] After the last supper He reassured His loyal, bewildered Eleven: "I will not leave you comfortless: I will come to you." [7]

Jesus gave hope to the sorrowing.

He gave hope, too, to the blind man at Bethsaida, and to a nobleman with a fevered son in Capernaum. He gave new life to ten lepers, as He did to the man with a withered hand, and the centurion's servant.

Jesus gave hope to the afflicted.

Perhaps the Master's greatest message was given on the Mount. There He told the meek that they would inherit the earth, and the pure in heart that they would see God. In the same Beatitudes, He extended everlasting hope, too, to the peacemakers, those persecuted for righteousness, the merciful and those who mourn.

Jesus gave hope to all men.

_____

[4] *Luke* 5:10.
[5] *John* 8:11.
[6] *John* 11:23.
[7] *John* 14:18.

"What can I do to make my life more exciting?" you may ask. Tonight I would suggest: Give someone *hope*. No gift will be more appreciated.

GLOW AND GROW

QUITE BY CHANCE, THE OTHER NIGHT
in thumbing through an old biography on George
Bernard Shaw, I stopped at the beginning of a chapter
entitled, "The Philosopher."

The book was written in 1909 by G. K. Chesterton,
the English artist who became a gingery essayist. The
chapter begins:

> "I should suppose that *Caesar and Cleopatra* marks about
> the turning tide of Bernard Shaw's fortune and fame. Up
> to this time he had known glory, but never success. He
> had been wondered at as something brilliant and barren,
> like a meteor; but no one would accept him as a sun, for
> the test of a sun is that it can make something grow." [1]

The remainder of the book I found disjointedly dull.
But that paragraph is a jewel.

Life's skies are full of flashing meteors. Then there
are some quietly powerful suns which make things grow.

Among the birds, few is better known than the
European cuckoo. A clock has been named for the
cuckoo, and William Wordsworth gave the bird further
fame as "a wandering voice." The cuckoo has enjoyed

_____

June, 1964
[1] Chesterton, G. K., *George Bernard Shaw*, New York, N. Y., John Lane Company,
  1909, page 165.

glory. But the European bird lays its eggs in others' nests. As a sun, the cuckoo is a failure. It does not even help its own eggs grow.

By contrast, one of America's best loved birds is the cardinal. More states — seven — call the cardinal their official bird than any other. Cardinals often build their nests among the brambles, and the brilliant red male is known for his attentiveness to his nesting mate. Cardinals have at least two broods of young in each nesting season. Quietly, tenderly, they help their young grow. Among birds, cardinals are suns.

There are streams that splash and roar spectacularly. But as a boy growing corn and tomatoes, I soon learned that it is a quiet trickle down an irrigation furrow that sinks into the good earth and helps young sprouts really grow.

Nothing on earth helps a boy or a girl grow more than a good mother. And the mothers I have found to be most successful are those who have moved with quiet, loving warmth. One of them I knew was as meek as a mountain violet. I never heard her raise her voice to her children. But she never slept until they were in at night. She prayed with them daily. She always had a ready bedtime story; and she taught them to love the scriptures, cherish the gospel, and seek honor. She was a sun.

There was another woman. I met her when she was in her late sixties. She wore a hearing aid. It was during World War II, and she was asked to teach a Sunday School class of restive boys and girls 12 and 13 years of age. They had not had a regular teacher for three years. Some of the children came from homes disrupted by war and other causes. Though this teacher was in her sunset years, in her was unbounded warmth and resolute courage.

She prepared long and hard — daily beginning at 6 a.m. When a boy was absent, she visited his home. She invited children to her apartment for help with assignments. Discipline came where there had once been disorder. Faith grew in young hearts which had been harassed with hatred. When that quiet woman died a few years later, there was an overflow crowd at her service. She [2] was a sun.

Of all the tributes I have heard at funerals, one which I perhaps remember best was paid by a banker to a former Congressman:[3] "Out in our basin, he helped hundreds of young men to say sincerely: 'I know that my Redeemer lives.' "

A neighbor woman [4] of ours has not been blessed with children of her own, but she with her husband is rearing four children from Greece — and carrying a full load in the Church.

There are cuckoos and cardinals, and roaring rivers and silent streams. There are meteors, and there are suns. There are men and women who find the fleeting glory of a shooting star. And there are those whose quiet glow helps others grow.

---

[2] May Broomhead Findley.
[3] Don B. Colton.
[4] Ruth (Mrs. Harry L.) Glick.

SWEET TOGETHERNESS

IT WILL NOT BE MANY WEEKS NOW before my favorite summer concerts begin. Their music I shall enjoy right from this old, blue-backed chair in my study where I sit tonight.

The concerts will come from the humble, unseen choir of crickets. "If moonlight could be heard, it would sound like that," Hawthorne said of their music.

Trouble is, their concert season never lasts long enough. It ends with the first frost. Then, almost all these little, dark-skinned musicians die — if they have not expired shortly before. (A new generation of crickets emerges each spring from the eggs the female buries with her spear-like tail.)

So, in a way, those cricket concerts are death chants.

But you would never know it. Their rhythmic chirps are cheerfulness itself.

When a heart is heavy, music can be a great comforter, particularly if it is enjoyed in a spirit of *togetherness,* like that of the crickets.

Walter Lord grippingly portrays the strength coming through music with togetherness in his book, *A Night to Remember.*[1] The book describes the sinking of the

April, 1960
[1] Henry Holt and Company, New York, N. Y., 1955.

Titantic in the North Atlantic on a cold April night in 1912. Some 1,502 lives were lost; 705 survived.

Shortly after the iceberg was struck, when passengers were not aware of a mortal blow, the ship's band began to play. As lifeboats were lowered, the band played on. Some musicians wore blue uniform coats; some, white jackets. Their beat was fast. The music was cheerful.

The band played as distress rockets shot into the starry sky, and the sinking ship began to look "like a sagging birthday cake."

The gay music continued as the cold, cruel sea crawled across a lower deck after the last lifeboat had been lowered, with hundreds yet remaining on the big ship.

As the reeling liner lowered deeper into the sea the band kept playing. The musicians now wore lifejackets over their overcoats.

At about the moment the bridge dipped under the waves and the sea rolled along the boat deck, Bandmaster Wallace Henry Hartley tapped his violin. The lively ragtime ended. The band began playing a hymn, "Autumn." As the Titanic's bow plunged deeper, the strains continued, until they were "buried in a jumble of falling musicians and instruments."

The author notes that generally the hundreds of passengers and crew who went down with the ship remained calm.

Music with togetherness was there as men and women met death with dignity and calmness and courage.

During World War II music with togetherness rallied battered, free men through "There'll Always Be an England." A century before, weary Pioneers had pressed on as together they intoned "Come, Come, Ye Saints."

Shortly after Pearl Harbor, the wife of a retired railroad president, Mrs. Walter S. Franklin, got an idea. A Red Cross Gray Lady, she took her little harp to hospitals. She played to despairing soldiers. To one youth, both eyes and his right arm below the elbow gone, she said: "Hi, Sam! You and I can make some music together." She put the fingers of his remaining hand on the harp's three buttons. Together they did "Comin' 'Round the Mountain." New hope glowed on that hospital cot.

The movement grew. Tens of thousands of patients were reached every year by Gray Lady music. Patients were encouraged to join in the melody. In a ward for policemen and firemen in a large Philadelphia hospital, two Gray Ladies approached a screened-off bed. One played their spinet piano. The other sang, "When Irish Eyes Are Smiling." A man's voice joined in. After it all, the head nurse volunteered: "Our man is going to live!"[2]

Strength through music with togetherness!

The other night, after Sunday service, I exchanged greetings with a woman [3] whose burdens I know are great. Her husband, a noble man, had been seriously ill for weeks. Her face was not beaming, but it was radiant. She had just finished singing in the choir. Her eyes, too, seemed to say, as the crickets seem to sing:

"There is strength through music with togetherness."

---

[2] Dutton, William S., "Why Not Music Like This in All Hospitals?" *Reader's Digest*, January, 1956, pp. 197-200.

[3] Mignon (Mrs. Norman J.) Astle.

TIMING

Our son Owen is short for his twelve years. He also has a freckled nose that is crooked. He will not say how it got that way. But it looks as though he had either been kicked by a horse or hit by a haymaker.

A few days ago we took Owen to a clinic to consult a specialist about straightening his nose.

"Yes, that nose needs fixing all right," the doctor said. "But I am going to recommend that we do not straighten it now."

Owen looked relieved. I looked puzzled.

"I am going to recommend that you make an appointment for straightening the nose three years from now, in April," the doctor continued. "With hospital facilities crowded as they are, that will give us several months to make arrangements. We should be able to do the surgery in June, when Owen is out of school."

"Why a three-year delay?" the doctor added. "There is a chance that if we do the surgery now the nose will cease to grow. I would not like to see Owen, as a man, with a Boy Scout's nose."

We got the message. Timing is important in straightening a boy's nose. Timing is important in much of life.

December, 1964

Patience is frequently the companion of good timing. So often we have moved when we should have waited. And then we have been sorry.

During the battle of New Orleans in 1815, fiery, hickory-tough Andrew Jackson realized the value of waiting, of timing. This was when the British lines were moving toward the Americans across cane stubble silvered by frost.[1]

Jackson ordered his men to cease fire to clear the view. As the enemy approached, Jackson instructed his men to aim above the plates of the white cross belts which latticed the enemy red tunics.

The red line, running now, reached within 300 yards of the Americans. But Jackson's men, many of them frontier sharpshooters, held their fire. Then the signal was given. A sheet of orange flame belched out. The fire continued. The silvery field of cane stubble was soon strewn with fallen redcoats. On that January 8, the British lost 700 men killed, 1,400 wounded, and 500 captured. Jackson's losses: seven killed and six wounded.

It was Andrew Jackson's finest hour. He became a national hero. In the battle of New Orleans he had waited for the right time, the right second.

Timing so often turns an incident into an event, brings success where defeat could have come.

The author of *Ecclesiastes* wrote: "To everything there is a season, and a time to every purpose under the heaven: . . . A time to rend, and a time to sew; a time to keep silence, and a time to speak." [2]

---

[1] James, Marquis, *The Life of Andrew Jackson: Part One: The Border Captain*, New York, New York, the Bobbs-Merrill Company, 1933, pages 243-247.
[2] *Ecclesiastes* 3:1, 7.

Timing is important in teaching, too. One of the most memorable lessons I ever received came when I was a boy of about ten. On a neighborhood street a construction crew was laying pipe. The joints were sealed with molten lead from a huge pot over a burning fire. One evening after the workmen had gone home, some of us boys dipped sticks into the pot of hot lead. After I pulled out my stick and allowed it to cool, it had the appearance of a small cattail with a head of lead on the end. I was proud of my trophy.

I was shaken later when someone said something about stealing.

That night we had a family home evening together in our home. My father told a story about an Arab boy leaving for a long journey. His mother gave him some money in a bag. Then she sewed the bag in the lining of his coat for protection against bandits. On the journey, the caravan was stopped by robbers. When the boy was asked if he had money, he said, "Yes." Then he explained that it was hidden in the lining of his coat. Impressed, the bandits commended the boy for his honesty and allowed him to keep his money.

After forty years, the story remains vivid to me. I shall ever be grateful to my father for waiting for the right time in my life to tell it.

I am going to look at Owen's freckled, crooked nose for many more days. Sometimes it may annoy me. But I hope it will remind me that there is a time for important moves, that patience is sometimes more powerful than action.

BOOK TWO
Fullness of Joy

*"Thou wilt shew me
the path of life:
in thy presence is fulness
of joy."*
—Psalms 16:11

COUNSEL FROM A COW

MANY A DAIRYMAN HAVE I KNOWN in my day. But never have I met one who appeared to love the cow like this genial gentleman from Illinois. Will A. Foster's [1] big body gestured happily as he talked of the cow's history and habits. His low, leathery voice literally fondled the word *cow* as he spoke it.

"The more I study her ways — and I have been doing it for 30 years — the more I find she is like people," he smiled.

He then told me that when a new cow is purchased by a dairyman, she is a wise one if she does not immediately move into the midst of the herd. "Rather," he said, "she will eat on the fringes of the herd until she is accepted. If she tries to move into the herd too soon, there usually is trouble."

Will Foster emphasized that the wise newcomer cow eats on the fringes for a while.

A man was named to a policy-making body in our city some years ago. From the start, in the meetings, he spoke up as long and loud as some of the seasoned veterans. We noticed he was soon facing feelings

————————

March, 1960.
[1] Special representative, American Dairy Association, and former vice president, Borden Foods Company.

against himself. He had not taken time to "eat on the fringes."

There is another man who recently was appointed head of an important organization. He moved in with a new broom which apparently began swinging too soon. He seemed to disregard his predecessor's policies entirely. Overnight he introduced new procedures. His organization was soon in confusion, and he in trouble. He had moved "into the midst of the pasturing herd too soon."

Joshua, who is said to have been a slave in Egypt's brick fields, became a mighty warrior-leader of Israel. In taking over after Moses' death, Joshua counseled his officers: "Remember the word which Moses the servant of the Lord commanded you. . ." The record says that twice more Joshua reminded them of Moses, in that command preparing Israel to pass over Jordan.

The men answered Joshua: "According as we hearkened unto Moses in all things, so will we hearken unto thee. . ."

Joshua seems to have won full acceptance sooner through leading his men in honoring the revered leader whom he had succeeded.[2]

A wise leader seems to take time to get the "feel" of his new call and to permit his people to get the "feel" of him.

Aneurin Bevan was a British political leader whose views often have been far from those of many Americans, including my own. But no one can deny that brilliant oratory helped Bevan win a post in Britain's cabinet

––––––––

[2] See *Joshua*, Chapter 1.

after World War II and also helped give him a powerful voice in his party over many years.

He once recalled how he as a boy of 17 in a Welsh mining town had a habit of stammering. He brought himself to confess his difficulty to Walter Conway. Conway, born in a workhouse, had risen to chairman of the South Wales Medical Society.

Conway answered: "You stammer in speech because you falter in thought. If you can't say it, you don't know it."

The Welsh boy decided thereafter to saturate his mind with every subject on which he was to speak or converse. He was interested in bettering working conditions of miners. He buckled down to long, hard study in his workman's library. He talked less and read more.

Bevan followed Conway's advice in his maiden speech in the House of Commons. His talk was not read. But his mind was brimming with his subject. After the speech, Winston Churchill of the Opposition came over to congratulate him. He liked his talk because it "was spontaneous — like a debater in rebuttal."

"If you can't say it, you don't know it," became rewarding watchwords through many years for Aneurin Bevan.[3]

To get back to that wise, incoming cow: she eats on the fringes until she is sure. Many men and women have climbed higher in doing likewise — whether joining a group, taking the helm or tackling a topic on which to talk.

————————

[3] Bevan, Aneurin, "The Best Advice I Ever Had," *Reader's Digest*, October, 1953, pp. 91-92.

WARRIOR'S WISDOM

HE HAD COMPLETED HIS PRESS CONFERENCE at the airport, and I was now driving him to a downtown hotel.

Captain Edward Vernon (Eddie) Rickenbacker had been questioned about subjects ranging from Cuba to Korea and from foreign aid to the federal debt. He had shot back with the tough frankness of a battle-scarred old warrior, which he is. He had backed his statements, often blunt and sometimes seemingly extreme, with impressive facts.

Now as we rode through the night, we chatted about his exciting past. It was only about a 15-minute drive, so there was little time for details: about his early days as an international automobile racing champion, his many brushes with death as America's air ace in World War I during which he shot down 22 enemy planes and four balloons, his pioneering as a peacetime pilot, his 18 years as owner of Indianapolis Speedway, Inc., his more than two decades as a successful president of Eastern Air Lines, and his harrowing experiences with seven others forced down in the Pacific during World War II and drifting for 21 days on three little rubber rafts.

September, 1963.

"Captain Rickenbacker," I asked, "of all your experiences, which do you think has been the most significant?"

He paused. Then reflected: "Well, I suppose I would have to say those days on the raft in the Pacific."

I recalled reading the installments of his account in our local newspaper 21 years before. I remembered how the seven men on the rafts (one of them had died at sea) had read the New Testament together and had held morning and evening prayers.

Then I said: "You must have really got close to the Lord during that experience."

His quick retort I hope my two sons, 10 and 6, will never forget. (They rode in the back seat.) "I was close to the Lord long before I was lost on that raft," he snapped. His leathery voice became reverent. "I don't wear my religion on my cuff. But it is there, deep. Every night I get down on my knees and thank God for the blessings of the day."

Our younger son kept tugging me with whispers. "Dad, give me a piece of paper," he repeated.

"Captain Rickenbacker, my boy wants your autograph," I said as we neared the hotel.

"I'm not going to give him an autograph," he growled. "He'll just lose the paper." Then he spoke as a kindly grandfather: "But I will send the boys something I think they might keep, copies of one of my books. When we reach the hotel, will you give me their names and address?"

I obliged, and the 73-year-old war hero, slightly stooped, limped toward the elevator.

Much of the next day we spent with the hard-driving

Captain. He moved through a long press conference and a civic luncheon (where his address drew a standing ovation).

He spoke admiringly of the Mormon Pioneers. "I flew last night in a jet over much of their trail," he said. "They were real men. They came on their own. They had no government subsidy."

About a week after we had bidden Captain Rickenbacker farewell, there arrived from his office, that of the chairman of the board of Eastern Air Lines, New York City, two copies of his *Seven Came Through*. Each book carried the boy's name with the Captain's signed greeting.

Together the boys and I have since been reading the story of that "most significance experience." In the book's introduction by W. L. White, we learned that Captain Rickenbacker became fatherless at 12; how, the day after the funeral, he got himself a job in a glass works for $3.50 a week.

We read how the Captain and his mates, thirsty and hungry and raw, writhed through long days under a searing sun, with sharks often bumping away at their small rubber rafts. We read of their many battles with the elements, with gnawing death. The Captain never lost faith that they would be rescued.

My sons should remember that story. I hope they will not forget the veteran warrior's example and statements on being self-sufficient, on not getting soft. Most of all, though, I would have them remember his words: "I was close to the Lord long before I was lost on that raft. I don't wear my religion on my cuff. But it is there, deep."

POWER IN A PENCIL

ON WHAT WAS ONCE A SLOPING GOLF fairway overlooking our city, workmen are now erecting a modern engineering building. It will serve our University.

The building has already been named: for a man who was teacher and leader at the University for 35 years. He was a plowboy who rose high. He earned a doctor of science degree as well as one for philosophy. He distinguished himself as engineer, educator, churchman and community builder. For years he was listed in *Who's Who in America*.

I never had him as a college teacher. But from him I learned some of my most valued lessons. They came in London, where he presided over the European mission of The Church of Jesus Christ of Latter-day Saints. For two years I served at headquarters under him. He is the late Joseph F. Merrill.

I do not recall his ever speaking about one of the unforgettable lessons he gave me. I received it by watching him, day after day, evening after evening. I can see him now at his desk, his broad, high forehead bent over a book, a magazine or a newspaper. His hair

————————

October, 1960.

was gray streaked with white. His was a rugged, earnest face, of rather tan-gray complexion, with a broad gray mustache. When he read he was as if in a world thousands of miles away. He read with a pencil, with blue lead, as I recall, and a pair of large scissors.

And that was his lesson to me: read with a pencil and scissors.

He read shelves of pages on nutrition, world affairs, theology, science and sports. And as he read, he always seemed to be looking for something. He filled file upon file with clippings marked by his reading pencil.

Ten years later he gave a series of radio lectures. They were interesting. They were scholarly. They were faith-building. They were convincing. Listener's demands brought them out in a book. As I read its pages, I could see in them much of that reading pencil and scissors.

Another man I know is a leading school administrator and churchman.[1] Many times I have been in meetings with him. Often he has been the presiding officer. But no matter where he is or who is speaking, he seems to listen with a pencil. On a slip of paper, he literally notes what he hears. That is perhaps a reason he has risen so high.

There lived another man whom I would like to have known. The son of a lumber mill operator, he was rejected from school at seven. His teacher explained: "He simply does not want to learn." His mother, granddaughter of a Revolutionary War captain, taught him to read and write. While still a youth he became a tramp telegrapher.

[1] Reed H. Beckstead.

He was considered rather odd among the carefree telegraphic crowd. His pay was good, but he wore cracked, scuffed shoes, ink-stained clothes and a tattered slouch hat. In the cold of winter he refused to buy an overcoat. Instead he bought scientific books and experimental apparatus. He also had a habit of carrying with him most everywhere he went — on the job, at the theater or at the dinner table — a pocket notebook. Into it he scribbled drawings and notes for experiments.

His name is Thomas Alva Edison, and it is said that in his lifetime he filled 2500 notebooks.

Edison seemed to think with a pencil.

For several reasons I am grateful they are erecting the Joseph F. Merrill Building at my alma mater. As I pass it, I hope it will keep reminding me: you will draw more from life if you read, listen and think more intently — with a pencil. You will give more to life, too.

SECRET OF HIS WISDOM

SOME NEIGHBORHOODS HAVE ONE.
Ours did. He was the unofficial neighborhood judge —
the man people went to with their problems.

It seemed all types went to that big-bodied, ruddy-
faced man for advice. There was the boy in the neighborhood who married at 17, and there was an elderly
couple with a Scotch twang who came to him from
across town. They say one father phoned him from
nearly a thousand miles away for counsel on handling
a wayward son. The mayor of our city was a caller.
So were the prison warden and the chief of police.

Some of us boys used to go to him, too.

Folks probably wondered where the secret of his
wisdom really lay.

People seemed to like him. We boys did, perhaps
because he would get down on his knees and shoot
marbles with us. He could fire his taw like a bullet.
He could hit shooting from a big ring, too. He taught
us boys how to knit our own baseballs from discarded
socks, and his front lawn was well worn from our
football games.

Neighbor folks could have gone to him for advice

February, 1961

because they liked him. But there were other men they liked, too. There was the fellow up the street who spent hours showing us how to collect stamps. There was the man with the crystal radio set. He would let us take turns putting on the earphones. There was another neighbor. He was pitcher on the high school team. We nearly worshiped him.

But we did not go to those neighbors for advice.

Through the years, others have probably wondered with me about the real key to that neighborhood judge's wisdom.

The other night I think I found a big part of the answer. A group of us were listening to a learned man from our university. He is an authority on family relations. He was answering our questions on how to counsel young people in trouble. "Be slow to give them advice," he said. "Listen them out. Listen with sympathy and understanding. Then help them to advise themselves rather than receive advice from you."

Since that talk, my thoughts have frequently returned to that neighborhood judge. I can remember problems that puzzled me: bullies to battle with, courses to choose at school, which job to take, and others. Some of these problems I took to him. But for the life of me I cannot recall any specific advice he gave me. I can remember, though, a line he often repeated: "Do your own thinking."

Yes, people probably sought his advice because he did not give it. Rather, he helped people administer it to themselves.

Apparently Solomon counseled that way. Remember how the two women came to him for a decision? They wanted him to decide which should have the babe. Both claimed to be its mother. Solomon asked for a sword. He ordered the child be divided, each woman receiving half. Then one woman pleaded: ". . . O my lord, give her the living child, and in no wise slay it. . ." [1] The other woman asked that the child be divided. There was then no question as to which was the true mother.

Wise Solomon let the two women make their own decision.

A man's free agency — his right to choose for himself — is a divine gift. That is why *no* advice is perhaps the best advice. Our neighborhood judge and Solomon would probably say it is better to help men advise themselves.

----

[1] *I Kings* 3:26.

SUGAR

YESTERDAY, MY WIFE, MARIAN, and I met an interesting new friend. She is a robust colored woman with broad, smiling lips. She stood beside a wall of colorfully gay straw beach hats and purses. Hers was a corner in the crowded straw market of Nassau, capital of the Bahamas. They are the string of islands, east of Florida, where Columbus is said to have first seen land in his discovery of America.

The woman wore a brown print dress and a bell-shaped straw hat trimmed with bright green. But she herself did not cause us to stop. What did were two dark brown coconut palm purses trimmed with white shells. Marian wanted them for our daughters.

There was no bargaining. We paid the price. The woman handed us the purses.

"Look," she said, rolling a purse with her large nimble hands as a newsboy does his paper. "These purses take little space in your luggage."

As we prepared to leave, she smiled. "Say folks, if you need any more purses or hats, will you ask for me. My name is Sugar."

Several hours later, we had decided to purchase a

March, 1961.

straw hat for our fourth daughter. We strolled down the rows at the straw market. Colored women beckoned to us. But we looked for Sugar. We found her, and Marian selected a light hat made from date tree straw and trimmed with yellow. It was shaped like a pagoda roof.

"Wouldn't you like me to sew her name on it with this pretty green?" Sugar asked. With a large needle, she stroked a long strand of green raffia.

"Thank you," said Marian, "but will you use yellow instead of green?"

Sugar sewed the name on the hat, admitting to us that she was 32 — "old on this island."

I asked the price. I expected to pay at least $2, since beach hats usually sold for $1.50 and the name should be worth 50 cents extra. Besides, with our daughter's name already on the hat, Sugar was sure of her sale.

Pridefully, she handed me the hat. Then smiled, "I make this to you for 50 cents—because you *remembered* me."

The more we enjoyed the island, the more we realized that Sugar's attitude was typical. Everywhere — in the quaint British shops, with the white-coated Bahama police, the fringed surrey taxi drivers, and drum-beating calypso musicians — we discovered here was *grateful graciousness.*

We found this grateful graciousness dramatically portrayed at Nassau's little Eden: Ardastra Gardens. Here were some fifty flamingos, national bird of the Bahamas. Graceful creatures, they were about five feet tall. Their long, thin legs and swan-like necks and bodies were a pink that became a rich orange at the head.

Their trainer and the owner of the gardens is Hedley Edwards, a husky, friendly colored gentleman. He told us it took 14 months to train this flock, known as Nassau's marching flamingos. "They are a shy and sensitive bird," he said. "But they like appreciation. The more generous your applause, the better they perform. Watch and see."

Then he led the birds into the parade ground. "Forward, march!" he called. The birds began marching, like the Queen's finest soldiers. The onlookers clapped hard, and the flamingos stepped higher. They marched even more magnificently.

It was an impressive spectacle, a moving demonstration of grateful graciousness, with a British flavor.

The historians will tell you that after Columbus walked ashore on the powdery coral shores of one of these islands, he knelt in gratitude to God for his discovery.[1]

I am thankful, too, for our discovery on these same islands. Sugar has it. The flamingos have it. All life in the Bahamas seems to throb with it. It is grateful graciousness.

---

[1] Morison, Samuel Eliot, *Christopher Columbus, Mariner*, New York, N. Y., The New American Library of World Literature, 1956, page 42.

KEEP THE FRECKLES!

TODAY I CHATTED WITH A VIBRANT little man of 53 with big freckles on his forehead all the way back to his receding reddish hair.

He was born in Austria, son of a struggling salesman of barber supplies. The red-haired boy left school at 15 to paint posters for a Vienna department store. Today he is known as Dr. Ernest Dichter, father of motivational research.

Dr. Dichter is founder and president of the Institute for Motivational Research, whose headquarters are a castle-like mansion of 30 rooms overlooking the Hudson River. The institute has branches in 15 countries, and a staff of trained psychologists and 3,000 interviewers.

Gesturing spiritedly, Dr. Dichter told us in detail of his findings in a nation-wide survey just completed on why people save money.

"There have been some changes in people's attitudes in recent years," he said. "This we have found through a thousand different interviews 'in depth' with people of various walks of life across America. They are not saving so much for a 'rainy day.' They are no longer saving to 'keep us with the Joneses.' They are saving

---

April, 1961.

to be more individualistic, to do things they would like — paint pictures, build boats, pursue learning and culture, travel, and to generally choose for themselves in a pursuit of inner happiness."

"Yes, people want to be more individualistic, be more themselves," he said. He related a typical comment: "All my doctor does for me now is get me well. I want more than a get-well pill. I want my physician to be more *interested* in me — like the good old family doctor. I want him to recognize me as an individual, not just another patient."

As the little doctor kept talking, I kept admiring those large freckles on his forehead. They underlined what he was saying. They seemed to say: "With all your learning and efficiency, don't lose your freckle-faced warmth and genuine interest in others as individuals."

A busy friend often telephones me at home. He is a successful man with many cares. Yet when our 4-year-old son answers the phone, there is usually a warm conversation for several minutes. They talk about everything — from toy trucks to what mother is preparing for dinner. Our boy loves it. He is being treated as a *somebody*, not as somebody's son. My busy friend has not lost his freckles.

Few men have given more freckles to the face of America and the world — than another reddish-haired man. He was born in a dusty little Missouri farm town. As a boy he attended church in a little log chapel which had a rough timber floor full of wide cracks. He once recalled that hogs slept under the floor; and when dogs got after the hogs, services were delayed until the disturbance was over. He gave to the world the story of his boyhood in *The Adventures of Tom Sawyer.*

Mark Twain, or Samuel L. Clemens, in his autobiography, gives a key to the source of many of his freckles. They came from his mother, Jane Lampton Clemens, his "first and closest friend." He describes her as a woman without a career, but with a character. She it was who used to sew on his shirts so he would not swim in dangerous Bear Creek.

Jane Clemens was a confirmed invalid at 40, yet she lived to be well past 87. Why? Mark Twain said it was because of her intense interest in others. "She had a slender, small body," he wrote, "but a large heart — a heart so large that everybody's grief and everybody's joys found welcome in it. . ." [1] He said she always found something to excuse, and often to love, in the toughest people. She even prayed fervently for the devil, Mark Twain recalled. He added that his mother once had 19 cats around the house. Some of them were former strays. He saw nothing of merit in any of them, except that they were unfortunate. And that was what was important to his mother.

Farm folks are becoming fewer. Automation is taking over in the home and office and plant and farm. Other such high-sounding influences as motivation research are guiding men's minds in much that they do. All this is well. But two wise men with reddish hair — Ernest Dichter and Mark Twain — would probably admonish us strongly: "With it all, don't lose your freckles!"

----

[1] Twain, Mark, *Mark Twain's Autobiography*, New York, N. Y., Harper and Brothers Publishers, 1934, page 116.

TWO STREETS IN ONE

We were on a hurried business trip through the towering Rockies of southwest Colorado. Our car rolled into the little mining town of Silverton. Resting on the broad, flat patch of land at 9,300 feet, Silverton is surrounded by bold, bare peaks which poke like massive arrowheads into the bright blue sky.

Our only call in Silverton was at its old newspaper office. The thin, ink-smeared publisher looked tired. He had a right to be. He was also the weekly's editor, reporter, advertising manager, typesetter, pressman, and circulation manager. But he greeted us warmly. He moved up toward the front of his shop, where a glass case displayed dusty samples of ore.

He was soon telling us about Silverton's interesting present and roaring past. "During the summer months, the narrow gauge railway train, with wooden coaches, makes a daily trip here from Durango, about fifty miles away," he began. "Most of the passengers are tourists. The local young men put on quite a show when the train arrives. They stage a simulated train robbery."

He continued: "Much of our town's colorful life occurs on what we call Blair or Empire Street. It was

---

February, 1963.

Blair Street in the early days. The street then was center of a gay mining town's unseemly side. Later, some nice homes were built on the other end of the street. The 'seemly' citizens who occupied them did not wish to have a Blair Street address. Their portion was named Empire Street. For some time the same street had two names: Blair for one end; Empire for the other."

Silverton's street is the story of two parts. So is your life and mine. So is the life of a friend of mine. When we first met, he was a gay young blade in college who often wore a white leather jacket and a haughty smile. He ran with a fast crowd. He seemed to care little about studies and less about making something of himself. "Blair Street" prevailed in his life. But a tip of "Empire Street" was there, too. On occasion he could be sincerely considerate of others.

Through the years I have watched that man work hard on his Empire Street side. It has inched upward. Blair Street has receded in the process. Today he holds a national reputation in his profession. His is an outstanding, close-knit family. He is a respected Church and community leader. His days are filled with selfless service. He is a happy man.

His life has been the story of Blair Street over again. The Silverton publisher told us how through the years the respectable side of the street kept growing, until the street became known as Empire for its entire length.

There was another friend who was an outstanding citizen, rich in achievement and friends. A reverse or two struck. He seemed to try to wash his troubles away with drink. His Blair Street kept growing. He died young, almost a forgotten man.

The other night a judge from Colorado spoke in our town. A ruggedly handsome man, he presides over Denver's juvenile court. He is Judge Philip B. Gilliam. He has heard more than 100,000 cases during his 25 years as juvenile and criminal court judge. He discussed young delinquents who came before him — characters in which the Blair Street influence kept growing.

"Every real delinquent I have handled has been a kid who did not like himself," the judge said.

How would the judge turn the growth to Empire Street in young lives? He would begin with their parents. "Perhaps the greatest single deterrent to juvenile crime would be for the mother and father of the boy or girl to love each other deeply," he said solemnly.

The judge would also instill within each youth a feeling of self-respect, self-importance, and self-love. "You never feel yourself as important as you should until you realize your relationship with God," he said.

The challenge to every man and woman is there in that Colorado street high in the mountain tops. A powerful key to meeting the challenge is in those words of the Colorado judge. I think my friend who has achieved so much after a Blair Street start would agree: Nothing keeps the Empire Street influence growing like a continuing realization of your kinship with Deity.

HE DID HIS HOMEWORK

JAMES MADISON WAS A COLORLESS WISP of a man. He was little over five feet, six inches tall and weighed not much over a hundred pounds. It was said that he never dressed in anything but black.[1] And he usually had but one suit at a time.

Heavy brows hung over his blue eyes. Washington Irving once described him as "a withered little apple-John." His talk was dry and often boring.

Some have said he really had no boyhood. He was not inclined toward sports. He was bookish. He was frail as a lad, and sickly as a young man. He was the eldest of twelve children. He was required to do little physical work amid the tall oak, cedars, and sumac — or among the peach and apple orchards — of his father's Virginia plantation. Toil was for the slaves.

There were twelve members of his graduating class at Princeton. Of them, Madison was the only one who took no part in the commencement exercises, except to receive his diploma. He was deeply interested in religion, but his weak voice kept him from the pulpit. He

---

July, 1963.
[1] Padover, Saul K., *The Complete Madison,* New York, N. Y., Harper & Brothers, 1953, page 8.

loved to study law. But he never became a lawyer nor passed the bar.

He was shy around women. At 31 he fell in love. Then his fiance broke off their engagement. He was a deeply wounded man. He was not married until he was 43, taking a widow as his bride.

He has never left an apt saying that has caught on with men. No anecdote about him has lived with the masses. His name is known, yet few men know his story.

But he was a chosen man. He was "raised up" by the Lord to a mighty purpose.[2] Most men would probably agree with his biographer, Irving Brant,[3] that more than any other man he shaped the present government of the United States of America.

James Madison, that colorless little man, was father of the Constitution.

Where lay Madison's greatness? First, he was a man with a pure heart. John Witherspoon, president of Princeton when Madison was a student there, knew him well. (The entire Princeton faculty at the time consisted only of the president and three tutors.) Dr. Witherspoon said of Madison to Thomas Jefferson "that during the whole time he was under his tuition he never knew him to do nor to say an improper thing." [4]

Jefferson, an intimate friend of Madison for fifty years, described him as a man of "pure and spotless virtue which no calumny has ever attempted to sully." [5]

James Madison was blessed with a brilliant mind and love of hard work. When momentous legislative contests

---

[2] *Doctrine and Covenants* 101:80.
[3] Brant, Irving, *James Madison* (in three volumes); New York, N. Y., The Bobbs-Merrill Company, 1941, 1948, 1950.
[4] Padover, *The Complete Madison*, page 3.
[5] Padover, *The Complete Madison,* page 6.

were fought, Madison generally won because he had done more homework than his foes. Sir August Foster, British minister to America, once wrote that Jefferson was more of a statesman and man of the world than Madison. "Yet the latter was better informed," Sir August added.[6]

Madison completed the regular course at Princeton in only two years. Often his sleep was but five hours a night. At only 24 he was elected to the Committee of Safety in Orange County, Virginia. Committees of this kind provided the local government at the time British colonial power was crumbling.

At 36, Madison represented Virginia at the Constitutional Convention. Some of the world's finest minds were at that convention. Among them were George Washington, Benjamin Franklin, Alexander Hamilton, and George Mason. When the convention's four months' work was completed, dry, scholarly James Madison emerged as the hero. He had drafted the Virginia plan for a union which foreshadowed the constitution which was finally adopted.

One of Madison's greatest triumphs came a year later. The Constitution was up for ratification by Virginia's convention. Opposing adoption were political giants Patrick Henry, one of America's great orators and governor of Virginia during the Revolutionary War; James Monroe; George Mason; and Richard Henry Lee. Madison led the forces in support of the Constitution. He debated the issues with Henry. Again and again the recorder of the debates made entries such as this: "Here

---

[6] Padover, *The Complete Madison*, page 9.

Mr. Madison spoke so low that he could not be distinctly heard." [7]

But Madison was armed with facts. Despite a mousy voice, he drove Patrick Henry and other opposition to the Constitution to defeat.

James Madison, a pure-hearted man, had done his homework.

———————

[7] Brant, *James Madison*, Vol. 1, page 100.

BIRDS IN THE BUSH

MY FRIEND [1] IS PUSHING 80 NOW. Yet he continues to talk excitedly about life. His business holdings are extensive. But he still enters new ventures with all the enthusiasm of a boy at his first ball game.

As several of us chatted the other day, he was asked about the key to his remarkable business success, his continuing youthfulness.

His brown eyes twinkled. He tilted back his bald, sun-tanned head and smiled: "You know, they say a bird in the hand is worth two in the bush. But I have always gone after the two in the bush."

He paused, then said: "May I give you an example? I got my start in business in Hurricane, a semitropical, little town in southern Utah. Hurricane is known for its red soil, fine orchards, and hot summers. Nearby is the Virgin River. Its waters become treacherous at times. I was in my twenties when I started a general store there. My business often took me to St. George — 31 miles away, the way most people traveled. That was the sure, safe way."

September, 1964.
[1] Charles B. Petty.

My friend continued: "But I did not take that road. I always took a poorer route. The road was twisted, rutted, and full of rocks and high centers. It wound over 'Purgatory Hill,' a real beast in a rainstorm. There was white clay at the bottom of the hill, then red clay, and was topped by a rocky ledge. The greatest hazard, though, was the crossing of the Virgin River."

He now spoke earnestly: "Yes, it was in many ways a terrible route. But it was eleven miles shorter. And it was always a challenge to me, particularly in crossing the Virgin. Once or twice my Model-T got stuck in midstream. Somehow I managed to get out. I learned, too, never to cross where the water was smooth. This meant sand had accumulated at the stream bottom. I found it was always better to cross in rough water. The sand would be moving there."

Is it not true that too often too many of us seek the safety of security instead of the adventure of the unknown? We cling fast to the bird in the hand. And the tighter and longer we cling the more we squeeze courage and creativity from our lives. The gray of fear moves in and rosy wonder fades.

Jacob's love of new horizons appeared to flag with old age. He seemed to hesitate about going down into Egypt to meet his long lost son, Joseph, after Joseph's brothers had found him, the Pharaoh's ruler.

On the journey to Egypt, Jacob paused at Beersheba, offering a sacrifice to God. The Lord there spoke to Jacob: ". . . I am God, the God of thy father; fear not to go down into Egypt; for I will there make of thee a great nation." [1]

---

[1] *Genesis* 46:1-3.

Robert N. Sears, vice president of Philips Petroleum Company, for years served as assistant to the late President Henry D. Moyle in the oil business. Bob Sears recently described how his boss kept pushing him into new challenges:

"In my early days in the oil business when I was helping to construct an oil refinery, and later when working in the refinery, every time Henry Moyle came to Spokane, which was about every three months, he would change my job. I often felt I should stay a longer time on some jobs, to get a little more experience. His remark to me was, 'You'll have to learn faster.' " [2]

There are more than two birds in the bush. The numbers are unlimited. Happy is the man who pursues them. Happier is he who pursues them with a courage fired by a faith in Him who spoke to Jacob at Beersheba: ". . . Fear not to go down into Egypt; for there I will make of thee a great nation."

---

[2] "Magnifying Our Potential," an address by Robert N. Sears at the concluding dinner, Brigham Young University Management Conference, Provo, Utah, June 5, 1964.

BOOK THREE

Enlarge My Steps

*"Thou hast enlarged
my steps under me,
and my feet did not slip."*
—Psalms 18:36

TIME FOR GREATNESS

WHENEVER SOMEONE HAS MENTIONED Daniel the Prophet, my thoughts have gone back to an old picture. It hung in my boyhood home. The brown print in a heavy frame, about three feet wide by two feet, portrayed Daniel in the lions' den.

Because of that vivid, exciting picture, Daniel was a childhood hero. But he was a hero in much the same sense as the lion tamer in Ringling Brothers' Circus, or Frank "Bring 'Em Back Alive" Buck.

Today, as I reread the Book of Daniel, Daniel emerges as an altogether new hero.

Daniel lived in momentous days — of shifting ideologies and tumbling empires. But he remained a king's ruler under several conquerors. Nebuchadnezzar, who destroyed Daniel's Jerusalem, elevated the pure-hearted son of Israel to be governor over all Babylon's wise men. Belshazzar, king of the Chaldeans, proclaimed him third ruler in the empire.

Belshazzar was slain, and Darius the Median took the kingdom. He set 120 princes over the land, headed by three presidents. Who was first of the presidents? Daniel.

––––––––

October, 1961.

Where was Daniel's greatness? He was selfless, courageous, wise, affable, and far-sighted.

But in three major crises in Daniel's life, I find evidence of another great quality — that of a master strategist. When harsh reverses came, *he asked for time.* Then he counseled with others, including his God. From each crisis he emerged in a stronger position.

Daniel's first test came shortly after he had been selected by Nebuchadnezzar's officials as one of the outstanding young captives to enter the king's court. The king had ordered that these young men be provided the ruler's own rich food and wine. Daniel balked. He wanted simpler fare, and water instead of wine. The official in charge explained that his own head could roll if instructions were not followed. Daniel faced a difficult decision. So *he asked for time* — ten days.

Daniel requested that he and his three companions be given simple food for ten days. Then their condition was to be compared with the others'.

Daniel won his point. He moved up another step toward greatness.

Nebuchadnezzar had his disturbing dream. But he forgot the dream. He asked his wise men to tell him the dream, then its interpretation. The reward if they delivered: rich gifts and great honor. The penalty if they failed: death.

The wise men failed. The order for death went out. Daniel was among those to be slain. To the king's captain asked to execute the order, Daniel inquired: ". . . Why is the decree so hasty from the king? . . ."[1] Then Daniel went to the king himself.

[1] *Daniel* 2:15.

Daniel asked for time. Given it, he counseled with his three companions. He prayed, too. The answer came. The king made Daniel a ruler.

Daniel's next recorded crisis came with Darius. The leaders whom Darius had placed under Daniel conspired against the Israelite. They asked the king to issue an unalterable decree. Under it, a subject petitioning anyone save Darius during a 30-day period would be cast to the lions.

Daniel was caught praying to his God. The word was passed to Darius. The king was troubled with himself. Here again, Daniel probably asked for time. And there is evidence that the time was used by Daniel to preach faith in his God to Darius. The king ". . . laboured till the going down of the sun to deliver him." [2] Then the king said to Daniel: ". . . Thy God whom thou servest continually, he will deliver thee." [3]

Daniel was unharmed in the lions' den, and Darius issued a decree requiring all throughout his kingdom to acknowledge Daniel's God.

Once again, Daniel had not panicked in a crisis. Rather, he had sought time. Then he had calmly and prayerfully and confidently prepared for the future. And Daniel conquered — again and again and again.

---

[2] *Daniel* 6:14.
[3] *Daniel* 6:16.

YOUTHFUL MATURITY

CONGO HAS BEEN BIG NEWS
in recent years. Of all the dispatches coming out of
that jumbled, jungle land, one particularly struck home
to me. It was the report of the death of a 31-year-old
American newsman in a skirmish between tribesmen and
Congolese soldiers. I did not know him, Henry Noble
Taylor. But I had, a few years ago, enjoyed a stimulating visit in our city with his father.[1]

Among the tributes to the young journalist was one
from Dwight D. Eisenhower. Another was an editorial
in the Scripps-Howard newspapers which he represented.
It said: "The career of Henry Taylor already was
brilliant, demonstrating a seriousness of purpose and
maturity of judgment far beyond his years."

"Maturity of judgment far beyond his years," is a
great tribute.

What makes a man mature in judgment — have the
ability to measure men and matters and movements with
a broad, solid rule?

A remarkably mature young mind belonged to a
nineteenth century German Jew. Son of a wealthy

January, 1961.
[1] Henry J. Taylor, former United States Ambassador to Switzerland and former net-
work radio commentator.

banker and grandson of a brilliant philosopher in the court of Frederick the Great, he was brought up in the Christian faith. He was a handsome youth: slender figure; big, black curls; dark, flashing eyes and a fetching smile. His mind and fingers twinkled like stars. At ten he began to compose music. At 13 he played his own public piano concerto. At 17 he conducted his own stirring overture to *A Midsummer Night's Dream*. He was dead at 39, with a loving family and the world of music deeply saddened at his passing.

Felix Mendelssohn was a genius in music. He also had a "maturity of judgment far beyond his years." When he was but 12, he visited the great Goethe. Felix wrote his mother this impression:

> "It does not strike me that the old gentleman's figure is imposing. He is not much taller than father; but his look, his language, his name — they are imposing. His hair is not yet white, his step is firm, his manner is mild. But the amount of sound in his voice is wonderful, and he can shout like ten thousand warriors."

At 14, Felix found an almost forgotten manuscript at his teacher's home that touched him deeply. It had been written by another German whose body had lain in an unmarked grave for 70 years. At 20, courageous young Mendelssohn decided to put the complicated work before the public. It called for two sets of orchestras and choruses. It was Johann Sebastian Bach's *St. Matthew Passion*. Mendelssohn's performance of it was a resounding success. Once again, the German Jew had proved himself a master in music, a mature young man in measuring greatness — even that which others had overlooked.

Brilliant, handsome young Mendelssohn for years continued to be the darling of Europe's concert halls. But apparently he would not let the tumult of acclaim go to his head. Biographers explain why. And in their explanation is perhaps the key to his maturity far beyond his years. He had been taught in his home "to realize the littleness of man in the greatness of the universe." He had also been taught to see his hopes and his achievements "in the framework of eternity." [2]

Early maturity came to Felix Mendelssohn in a large measure, apparently, because he learned to weigh life continually on the scales of eternity as against the hour.

Mendelssohn's broad outlook no doubt was further strengthened by his study of Bach. On the margin of many of his scores, Bach scribbled: "To God alone the glory." Elbert Hubbard said of Bach: "He knew his kinship with divinity so well. . ." [3]

To realize continually that you are the child of God is to give you personal dignity. And dignity begets maturity.

The heaving world today, more than ever, seeks men and women with maturity of judgment. To help develop it, Felix Mendelssohn would probably suggest, with sweet music in his voice: continually see life in the broad framework of eternity, not forgetting who you really are — a child of God.

---

[2] Thomas, Henry and Dana Lee Thomas, *Forty Famous Composers,* Garden City, New York, Halcyon House, 1948, page 97.
[3] Hubbard, Elbert, *Little Journeys to the Homes of Great Musicians,* East Aurora, Erie County, New York, Roycrofters, 1901, page 136.

WHEN A BOY BECOMES A MAN

OUR OLDEST SON IS JUST 7. He is pint-sized and not particularly fond of fighting. But he has two front upper teeth missing, and he likes his light brown hair crew cut.

Like most boys his age, he is hard on Levis at the knees. He spends hours with his red plastic building blocks. Only the past year he has developed a taste for baseball and basketball. He bats around a white plastic ball with holes in it, and for basketball he bounces a big green rubber ball through the house.

A few weeks ago I propositioned him. If he would keep the household wastebaskets emptied, this summer we would build him an outdoor basketball standard on the dirt clearing by our home.

The boy's gray eyes twinkled; the wastebaskets were emptied fast. But as the weeks wear on, I find at times the wastebaskets in the kitchen and bedroom brimming over. They are usually emptied fast when I remind our boy. But, periodically I have to keep reminding.

Our lad is still a boy. But someday — not too far away, I hope — he may become a man.

––––––––

June, 1960.

When *does* a boy become a man? There have been all kinds of answers. They used to tell us a boy becomes a man when his voice begins to squeak, or when he first uses a razor; or when he starts paying an adult fare on the bus or at the theater.

But I disagree. A boy becomes a man when he takes a job and sees it through — without an overseer. He performs and deports himself as well when he is alone, or away, as when his superior stands nearby. He is his own policeman.

Yes, there are men who are still boys, and there are boys who have become men. At least with his job, our newsboy is a man. Our paper is always there, come heat or high snow, and the snow really comes high out our way.

As a business venture, the Pony Express a century ago failed. Its owners lost $200,000 and went bankrupt. But the Pony Express gave to the world a thrilling chapter on boys who were men. They were the youths who rode the Express, often wearing a red shirt, blue trousers and a buckskin jacket. Some were in their teens. Few weighed over 125 pounds.

Alone, those boys who were men rode their missions. Often they met blizzards and numbing cold, swollen rivers, a searing sun or flying arrows. But they rode on with the mail. There were fellows like young Robert Haslam. They called him "Pony Bob." Once after making his regular ride of some 75 miles, he found no rider nor horses at the station to relieve him. Indians had been there. He rode 65 more miles. He mounted a fresh horse and continued. He found another station burned to the ground. He rode on and on to headquarters. All in all he completed 380 miles in 36 hours. Alone, he finished his mission. "Pony Bob" was a man!

Norman Rockwell has been called "the most famous and best loved of American artists." [1] None has portrayed the American scene like Rockwell — the old swimming hole, country cousins, hatpin grandmothers, freckled Boy Scouts and many others. Rockwell is a great illustrator. But as you get into his autobiography you realize that he is greater because he early became a *man* in a creative profession in which it is not always easy. While he worked alone he disciplined himself to meet deadlines. He tells how as a young illustrator he devised for himself a system for creating ideas — when he felt he had run out of ideas. He would eat a light meal, sharpen twenty pencils and spread pads of paper across the dining room table. Then he drew a lamppost. For hours he drew random situations that came to his mind, starting with a lamppost. And that was the beginning of a new *Saturday Evening Post* cover drawing.

Since he was 22, Norman Rockwell has drawn over 300 *Post* cover subjects — representing a lot of deadlines for a creative man who as a youth learned to police himself as he toiled alone.

To get back to those wastebaskets, someday I may find them no longer brimming full. When and if that day comes, it will be a happy one. Then we will know:

Our boy has become a man!

---

[1] See Rockwell, Norman, "My Adventures as an Illustrator," *Saturday Evening Post,* Feb. 13, 1960, pp. 19-21, 109-112.

THEY MADE OTHERS KINGS

IT HAS NEVER BEEN A WISH OF MINE to live in any but this wondrous age. But I would like to have dropped in for just one day on the eighth century before Christ. All I would have wanted then was the privilege of a visit with one man.

He was a practical man whose lips were a well of wisdom, whose eyes could see for centuries. He lived when Rome was born. He himself was probably born in Jerusalem, son of Amoz. He was well schooled, and was adviser to kings. He was a poet, too, and a family man. He was a prophet. He has been called "prince of prophets." His name was Isaiah.

This great prophet foresaw, more than seven centuries before the event, the coming of Him whom Isaiah called the Prince of Peace. Some of our most inspiring lines on Jesus today come from Isaiah. Handel's *Messiah* is full of Isaiah, word for lofty word.

Near the close of the book we know as Isaiah, the prophet tells of a rebellious people, "a people that provoketh me to anger." These were a people "which say, Stand by thyself, come not near to me; for I am holier than thou." [1]

October, 1959.
[1]*Isaiah* 65:3, 5.

Isaiah himself no doubt was a humble man. He once described himself as "a man of unclean lips." [2] Perhaps that is why he had so much contempt for the "holier-than-thou" attitude.

There is a temptation to all of us to set ourselves above some others. There are those who seem to think their position or birth makes them more righteous. Some of us, overlooking our own shortcomings, at times look down on men who may have faults that do not happen to be ours. We are prone to wear our "goodness" as a badge of rank.

But wise Isaiah advised, in place of those attitudes, a life that would "learn to do well; seek judgment, relieve the oppressed," [3] and help the widow and fatherless. He seemed to say that we should always strive to enthrone others rather than ourselves.

A man who seemed to have every right to exalt himself was Alfred. He lived about the same number of years after Jesus as Isaiah had before. Alfred was the son of royalty. He himself became Britain's only king who has been called "the Great." He came to the throne in 871. He has also been called "father of the British navy." He was a brilliant warrior who repelled the formidable Danes in days when men fought with swords and arrows, and warships were powered by oars. He built cities and promoted industry. He framed a code of laws that was basis for later codes. He has been called an "English Solomon." He was a scholar and an author. He is credited with three important translations from Latin to Anglo-Saxon, including Bede's famous *Ecclesiastical History of England.*

[2] *Isaiah* 6:5.
[3] *Isaiah* 1:17.

But more than all that, history records that Alfred was a dedicated Christian, who lived a "life of quiet virtue." It is said that he "lent the weight of a great name and a stainless reputation to the fine theory that public office is a sacred trust." [4]

Legend tells of Alfred, hiding out at one time in a peasant's home, accepting the scolding of the peasant's wife after the king had let her biscuits burn. Another tale tells of his disguising himself as a harper and entering the enemy Danish camp to learn their secrets. These may be folklore, but they probably give a key to the character of a king who seemed to try to make all his people kings — quietly.

Only this past week I picked up in our study a magazine my wife had been reading. It tells of a struggling couple paying off a big debt caused by a business reverse. They had three children and another on the way. They read in their newspaper of a blond, blue-eyed boy of four who wanted a mother and father to "love and care for him." The boy was totally blind. They adopted him, after a conference with their children. Then follows a five-page account of their trials and triumphs, the jolts and joys in bringing the blind boy into the family circle.

I am not an emotional fellow, but I tugged with the tears after getting into that story. It seemed to say so powerfully, so touchingly, what Isaiah had said, and Alfred had shown, about the life to lead as opposed to "holier than thou."

———————

[4] Lees, Beatrice Adelaide, *Alfred the Great, The Truth Teller*, New York, N. Y., G. P. Putnam's Sons, 1915, page 426.

IF WE WANT TO WIN

MY FRIEND [1] HAD JUST RETURNED from a trip to Africa. He had enjoyed a picture-taking safari. He had watched lions sleeping off a meal of zebra. He had seen giraffes and elephants and hyenas — and a large group of baboons. Through the night he had peered down on big game from the famed Tree House near the slopes of towering Mount Kenya.

But he spent little time telling us about Africa's wild life. Rather, he talked excitedly about mining operations in Orange Free State.

Young colored men from various parts of Africa's back country are flown in to work in the mines. "We saw a group of employees representing thirty different languages and dialects," my friend said. He explained that, at the mines, they are taught a common language. They are provided good housing and excellent hospital facilities in a new, planned community of approximately 100,000 people. The city is called Welkom. There are approximately 30,000 employed in the mining operation. They bring out gold from shafts penetrating the earth from 8,000 to 12,000 feet — more than two miles down!

———————

February, 1962.
[1] George S. Eccles.

These young men from the bush in Africa work in the mines on a contract for one to three years. Then they usually return to the back country, purchase a wife, and resume tribal life.

As we listened, we were impressed with the good these gold mines are doing for peace and understanding in Africa, a continent coming before the world so often through headlines of war and strife and unrest.

Tribesmen from far and near come together, toil and live and play together, and then return to their respective peoples.

What started this interesting operation for peace? I do not know the beginnings of those gold mines. But they probably started because some free, bold man was willing to take the risk of drilling a costly hole into the desert in hopes of finding a ribbon of gold. And he found it deep down where the heat is unbearable without air conditioning.

Recently a machine tool manufacturer published an advertisement [1] headed:

"If We Want to Win,

We Have to Risk Losing."

The copy went on to say: "Nothing worth having is ever won by weakly pecking at it, by being afraid of it." Freedom began in America, the advertisement noted, by a people willing to risk everything: "our lives, our fortunes, and our sacred honor."

I have watched wild young geese learning to swim along the banks of the Green River, in an untamed area of the Rockies. These goslings risked drowning to learn to swim.

[1] Warner & Swasey, Cleveland, Ohio, in *U. S. News & World Report*, July 30, 1961.

I have seen a fluffy black cub stumble up a young pine. He risked a bad fall to learn to climb higher.

Almost everyone has watched a speckled young robin learning to fly. He risks a crash as his quivering wings stretch out.

But the wild goose enjoys more freedom as he swims, the bear as he climbs, and the robin as he wings into the blue. Because all ventured boldly, they achieved. And because they achieved, they also won new freedom from enemies which would destroy.

Freedom is a priceless gift — for a wilderness goose, a tribesman in Africa, or a man toiling with a diesel engine in Cleveland. But freedom has a price. It is a willingness to venture, to accept risk in place of security. It is a readiness to risk all, if necessary, for the soul-deep peace which only freedom under God can give.

This week a woman [2] I know is undergoing heart surgery. The operation, she told me, is her choice. "I have children to raise," she said in her hospital room. "I could probably stay with them for some time, as a semi-invalid. But if I remain, I want to remain in a condition to really mother them."

She had probably never read the advertisement's headline. But as she resolutely faced death, she eloquently showed me the meaning of the message:

"If we want to win,
We have to risk losing."

--- --- --- --- ---

[2] Mrs. Dan S. (Phyllis) Gardiner, Jr.

TOP DOG

THEY SAY THERE ARE SOME 24 MILLION dogs in the United States. The census takers too will tell you that the dog population is increasing almost twice as fast as the human population (15 as against 8 per cent in the previous five years).

The American Kennel Club recognizes 113 breeds of dogs. Among them are the kingly Danes. We used to call them Great Danes. We had one years ago, and he was like a pony running through the house and around the yard. Then there are the gallant collies, made even greater favorites by Albert Payson Terhune's *Lad: A Dog*, and Eric Knight's *Lassie Come-Home*.

And among the nation's dogs are the beagles, said to be currently the most popular of all breeds, according to Kennel Club registrations; the tough-looking boxers, the sad-eyed but lovable cocker spaniels, the prim poodles and many others.

Historians will tell you, too, that dogs have been favorites for not only centuries, but for millenniums. The Egyptians used dogs like our modern greyhounds to hunt antelopes. The Romans had for pets large mastiff-like dogs. There are over twenty references to dogs in the Bible.

—— —— ——

May, 1960.

The bulldog was developed in Queen Elizabeth's time to take part in the then popular sport of bull-baiting. Foxhounds rose with fox hunting in Britain and were sent to colonial America.

I recall a stately statue to his dog on the grounds of the castle-like home of Sir Walter Scott in southeastern Scotland.

Yes, dogs have held a high place in history.

There have been and are today dogs of courage, companionship and consequence — millions of them. But recognized everywhere as America's top dog in 1960 was a little mop of reddish hair standing only 8½ inches high and weighing only 9½ pounds.

He was an English-bred Pekingese, and his name was Chik T'Sun of Caversham. He reigned as the country's top dog because of his triumph as best-of-show in "the World Series of dogdem," the Westminster Kennel Club show, in New York's Madison Square Garden.

While this was the first victory for a Pekingese at the Garden, the breed is not new. In fact, it is probably one of the oldest. It is said that even before Moses led the Israelites from bondage the Chinese kept "lion dogs" similar to the modern Pekingese, which were brought to the outside world by a British admiral in 1860.

How and why did the little Peke win best-of-show? There are many reasons. One of them is that he, thanks to an able handler, repeatedly *showed his best*. His handler was tiny Clara Alford, half-Cherokee from Oklahoma. She carefully fed him chopped steak with wheat germ, and brushed his flowing hair from two to nine hours a day. The Peke was denied many of the pleasures of most dogs, such as romping with children or other dogs, to avoid eye injury. In her station wagon, Clara carried him from dog show to dog show. (He had won a record 126 "best-in-shows" before the Westminster.) At each motel she carefully selected a smooth stretch of grass for his six-foot exercise pen, free from twigs of briars which might snag his hair. Just prior to his final effort in the Westminster ring, she gently sprayed his coat with water, to quiet the hair — "there's so much electricity in it."

Then the little Peke took over. He moved across the floor with "stature" in a controlled roll. He again showed for his handler "as if born to the purple," in the words of the New York *Times*. He won the judge's nod as best-of-show, ahead of a broad-chested bulldog, a lively Pembroke Welsh corgi and 3,544 other dogs in the show. The huge crowd loved it.

The Peke, though only a mite, had with his handler apparently given his all. And it was enough — enough to become top dog for a year among America's millions!

GIVE YOURSELF A SPUR

It was one of the exciting experiences of the year for me. We were interviewing top students from 13 high schools for a scholarship award.

We asked them what they read, not required by school. We asked each to name his hero or heroine, and tell why. Lincoln was the most popular choice. But one named Albert Schweitzer, and another, George Marshall. A girl picked Eleanor Roosevelt.

One of the students herself became a heroine for me. She did not win the award. But I shall long remember her answer to the question: "What has motivated you to achieve so much?"

Blue-eyed and blond, she answered directly, modestly, and sincerely: "I have but one brother, no sisters. He is retarded. I am trying to make a contribution for him as well as for myself."

Most everyone has a goal, or goals, in life. Some of us achieve them. Some do not. One of those young scholars told us his aim was to become a United States Senator or justice in the Supreme Court. He will probably come closer to achieving his ambition if he couples it with a spur — something to keep pushing him upward toward his goal.

October, 1962.

In space travel, they call it thrust. That girl had it. She had given herself a spur: to make up for a brother she loved.

William Allen White was a country editor who became a mighty influence in America before his death in 1944. After his death he was awarded a Pulitzer prize for his autobiography.[1] In it he describes the event from which he drew a spur. His father had been dead for three years. Bill White at 17 was away to college. His mother kept boarders to maintain him there. Both of Bill's roommates were putting themselves through college. One was janitor in a bank; the other, a printer.

From them, Bill White took his spur. No longer would he lean on his mother. He would put himself through college. He wrote three letters to his hometown of Eldorado, Kansas. One went to the proprietor of a dry goods store; another, to a groceryman; the third, to the town's newspaper editor. White asked each for a job. The editor responded with an offer. And William Allen White had found his life's work!

The Apostle Paul told the Corinthians how a "thorn in the flesh" had become his spur. He added how he learned to ". . . take pleasure in infirmities, in reproaches, in necessities, in persecutions, in distresses for Christ's sake: . . ."[2] From them, Paul explained, he took strength. From each he apparently found a spur.

When I was a boy, people talked a great deal about a book, *The Americanization of Edward Bok*.[3] It is the

_____

[1] White, William Allen, *The Autobiography of William Allen White,* New York, N. Y., The Macmillan Company, 1946.
[2] *II Corinthians* 12:10.
[3] Bok, Edward William, *The Americanization of Edward Bok*, New York, N. Y., Charles Scribner's Sons, 1924.

autobiography of a Dutch immigrant boy who rose to become a great editor of *The Ladies' Home Journal.* Through the book you find a series of reproaches or necessities from which Edward Bok drew spurs to thrust him higher in achievement.

In Holland, Bok's mother had servants. But in America, with her husband's fortune in investments lost, she found herself in ill health with considerable housework. Young Edward and his brother came to her rescue. They scrubbed, washed dishes, and prepared meals. From circumstances like this, Edward drew a spur to achieve — to bring to his mother the comforts she had known in Holland.

A brilliant son of a multi-millionaire was, his family believed, headed for a career as writer or teacher. Then, his older brother Joe was killed in World War II. Joe was going to be the family's politician. From Joe's death, his brother took a spur. He would enter politics. That younger brother became President John F. Kennedy.[4]

Rich or poor, every man can find in his experiences something to spur him toward his dreams, to give him greater capacity, to drive him upward and onward. That is what a blue-eyed high school girl seemed to say to me when she answered: "I am trying to make a contribution for him as well as for myself."

---

[4] See biography of John F. Kennedy, *The World Book Encyclopedia*, Vol. 10, Chicago, Illinois, Field Enterprises Educational Corporation, 1962, pages 2, 3b.

"HE HELD HIS SPEAR"

A YOUNG EXECUTIVE FRIEND CAME TO ME bristling with fury toward his close associate, a member of his staff.

"He gossips too much," the young leader said. "He stirs up trouble."

My friend was really upset. He was in a mood to dismiss his subordinate.

The incident reminded me of times I had felt the same way, more often toward a superior than a subordinate. I also recalled some advice I had once received: "Never make a major decision when you are upset with anger or depression — or heady with ecstasy."

That lesson was learned bitterly by a great leader one night in the fortress of Samarkand. It was situated in what is now southern Russia, near the high peaks bordering Afghanistan. On that night some 2,300 years ago there was a gay festival in the fortress. The center of the celebration was Alexander, Macedonian conqueror yet in his twenties. The great Persian Empire had been his latest prize. Guests sang praises to Alexander. They even exalted him to the stature of the gods. The young conqueror's ecstasy seemed to rise higher with each strain of acclaim.

———————

April, 1963.

Then his friend Clitus, drunken from wine, spoke up against the blasphemy. He reminded Alexander, too, that he, Clitus, had previously saved the conqueror's life in a battle with the Persians at the River Granicus. Alexander, frenzied with rage, made a decision. He grasped a spear from the hands of a guard. He hurled the spear at Clitus. The spear found its mark. Alexander's childhood friend, his companion in conquest, and his rescuer fell with the mortal blow.

Mighty Alexander was grief-stricken. For a day and a night, he writhed in anguish and remorse. He refused food and drink for days. One of his biographers wrote: "A man who aspired to rule the whole world had shown himself unable to rule his own temper." [1]

Too many of us hurl the spear of a major decision when our minds are flush with anger, despair, or ecstasy.

Esau, Isaac's firstborn and favorite, made a major decision when he was gaunt with hunger. His depression dimmed the luster of his priceless birthright. Esau reasoned: "Behold, I am at the point to die: and what profit shall this birthright be to me?" (*Genesis* 25:32.)

And when his mental lights were low, Esau sold his birthright for some bread and pottage of lentils.

I once knew a young man of ability starting off a career in his chosen profession. He toiled hard and was making progress. Then reverses struck. One discouraging day he hurled his spear. He submitted his resignation without another position to accept. He was sorry.

Your newspaper is full of headlines over stories resulting from spears hurled in passion. They have been

_____

[1] Wheeler, Benjamin Ide, *Alexander the Great*, New York, G. P. Putnam's Sons, 1911, pages 407, 408.

tossed from upset lovers, from misty-eyed men and women temporarily discouraged, or from others blinded by anger. Some are golden spears hurled in a moment of sweet victory or adulation. And golden spears — decisions made when spirits are heady and high — can be as damaging as the cold spears of depression or the hot spears of temper.

Perhaps the words of Maharbal, an ancient cavalry commander, are a caution to us all. To his leader, the great conqueror from Carthage, Maharbal said: "You know how to win a victory, Hannibal, but not how to use one." [2]

My young executive friend held his spear. He let his decision wait until his mind was calm. I have since watched him grow in stature and climb in station.

---

[2] Allen, John, *One Hundred Great Lives*, New York, N. Y., The Greystone Press, 1945, page 273.

LIONS AMONG MEN

TODAY MY EYES CAME TO A HALT OVER AN UNUSUAL magazine article: "The Ten Best Managed Companies."[1]

The magazine had asked some 300 business leaders to select from the thousands of companies in American industry those which they consider the best managed. The article lists the top ten,[2] then summarizes the reasons each was selected. American Telephone and Telegraph Company was chosen for its "corporate vitality," and General Motors Corporation for "organization." Sears Roebuck & Company was selected for "performance and planning."

But as I scan the strengths of all these ten great corporations, I find one quality which keeps cropping up. It is *boldness.*

Standard Oil (New Jersey), for example, in the 1930's bought properties in Venezuela, and in the 1940's became the first American company to venture into Arabian fields. Following World War II, Sears Roebuck made a move most other merchandisers feared to take.

November, 1963.

[1] *Dun's Review and Modern Industry,* Dun & Bradstreet Publications Corporation, January, 1963, pages 32-36, 79-87.

[2] The ten companies selected: American Telephone & Telegraph, du Pont, Eastman Kodak, General Electric, General Motors, International Business Machines, Minnesota Mining & Manufacturing, Proctor & Gamble, Sears Roebuck, and Standard Oil (New Jersey).

They expanded into as many newly located outlets as possible.

Proctor & Gamble has plunged heavily into television advertising to presell its soaps and detergents.

Boldness seems to pay in business. It has brought rich rewards in other pursuits, too.

As I reread the life of that tentmaker of Tarsus who became one of the greatest missionaries of all time, Paul's boldness keeps shining out from his stormy path. To the Ephesians he wrote of his burning desire to ". . . speak boldly, as I ought to speak." [3] Barnabas, taking Paul to the apostles after his conversion, told them how Paul ". . . had preached boldly at Damascus. . ." [4]

Paul's boldness glistened in the prison that night after he and Silas had been beaten with stripes. At midnight the two "sang praises unto God." Before morning the jailer had been baptized. Paul spoke out boldly on the "Unknown God" at Mars Hill in sophisticated Athens. He perhaps was never so bold as that day he defended himself before King Agrippa, and the king said: ". . . Almost thou persuadest me to be a Christian." [5]

Paul was humble, but he was a bold giant among men.

When newsmen in our town talk about the masters of the past, they often dwell on the name of a thin, quiet, but quick and humorous city editor named Alfred Pierce Reck. He was plain Al Reck to friend and foe.

Al Reck was acclaimed one of the nation's most able newsmen after he completed 27 years as city editor for

---

[3] *Ephesians* 6:20.
[4] *Acts* 9:27.
[5] *Acts* 26:28.

the Oakland *Tribune*. One of his reporters recalled this typical story [6] of his determined boldness:

It was Saturday night, and Al Reck phoned the city desk from home for any developments. He was told of a dying boy in town whose last wish was for some fresh peaches. They were out of season, and his mother had placed a classified advertisement in Reck's newspaper. There had been no response.

"Get the kid some peaches," said Reck.

Amateur radio operators were alerted. The word ticked out over the air: "Are fresh peaches in season there?" Some fresh peaches were located in New Zealand. Arrangements were made for an airline to rush them to Oakland without cost.

Then came a disturbing hitch. Governmental rules would not permit fresh fruit to enter the country without complicated clearance.

Told of the problem, Reck snapped, "We'll see about that." It was 3 a.m. in Washington, D.C.; but he phoned there at his own expense, tracking down a Department of Agriculture official. The peaches were cleared in 15 minutes. The dying boy received his wish, and Reck's newspaper published a stirring human interest story. But at his request, there was no mention of his role.

The boldness of Paul in the city room!

"Bold as a lion" [7] is a scriptural tribute to a truly righteous man. Today the world calls for lions among men.

---

[6] See Martinez, Al, "City Editor Reck of the Tribune," *Editor & Publisher*, July 6, 1963, pages 12, 48, 49.
[7] *Proverbs* 28:1.

BOOK FOUR

Restoreth My Soul

*"He restoreth my soul:
he leadeth me in the paths
of righteousness
for his name's sake."*
— Psalms 23:3

WINGS FOR YOUR HOPES

THE MAN WHO OPERATES THE DOWNTOWN public garage where I park my car held a sheet in his hand. He chuckled loudly as he commented to us about its contents.

"It says here that Benjamin Franklin thought it would probably take centuries to settle the American continent," he called. "And listen to what Thomas Jefferson said when he announced the Louisiana Purchase. He predicted that the territory would likely be fully occupied after 25 generations."

The garage man continued: "They were great men, but they surely missed on those predictions. They were far too conservative."

He handed me the sheet.

It was *Brevits*,[1] published for investors. My friend had been commenting on excerpts on the sheet from observations by Crawford H. Greenewalt, until recently president of E. I. du Pont de Nemours & Co.[2] Mr. Greenewalt cited other instances of short views on tall

---

January, 1963.

[1] *Brevits*, published biweekly by Vance, Sanders and Company, Inc., Boston, Mass., Sept. 10, 1962 issue.

[2] From an address, "Let's Take the Long View," given by Mr. Greenewalt before the Commonwealth Club of California, in San Francisco, Jan. 22, 1954.

subjects. The economist Jevons in 1860 was concerned at the possible exhaustion in a few years of the earth's coal supply. In the early 1900's, a Philadelphia man enthusiastically foresaw the time when there would be "a hundred motorcars or so" in every city.

The article in *Brevits* was entitled: "Always Underrated."

Wise men have underrated the potential of their fellow men. Most men and women underrate themselves. You can achieve much more than you think.

Remember the farewell of Jesus to His apostles? He and the Twelve had completed the Last Supper. The Master had dipped the sop and had given it to Judas Iscariot. And Judas had departed into the night on his dark mission. Comforting the Eleven, Jesus said in His Father's house were many mansions. He described the oneness in purpose of the Father and Himself. Then the Master, nearing His earthly sundown, spoke these great words for every man:

"Verily, verily, I say unto you, He that believeth on me, the works that I do shall he do also; and greater works than these shall he do. . ." [3]

What greater promise for himself could a man desire?

Few statesmen have touched me with speech as did Everett McKinley Dirksen, Senator from Illinois. He spoke in our town many years ago, but his words linger to this day. On another occasion, Senator Dirksen spoke on Abraham Lincoln. The Senator described Lincoln as "an instrument of divine destiny." Continuing Senator Dirksen said: "History is but the unfoldment of a divine pattern."

[3] *John* 14:12.

Everett Dirksen seemed to realize as a fatherless farm boy his own destiny. His mother's struggling family lived in the "Beantown" section of Pekin, Illinois. There, frugal immigrants grew beans instead of flowers. Young Ev helped grow and sell lettuce, turnips, and onions. Much of each Sunday was spent with the Bible. Some of Ev's greatest fun came when it rained. In the family barn, he nailed old boards into a platform. Then he would climb on it and start preaching to himself.

Young Ev's eyes looked beyond the barn walls. They could no doubt see the halls of Washington. Perhaps his thoughts took wings from the words of Jesus.

A few days ago a friend spoke to me of a man who has stirred him to greater heights: "He always made me feel I was so much better than I was, but I have tried to live up to his expectations of me." My friend continues to rise as a leader among men.

Most every man has within him so much more power and potential, ability and divinity than he realizes. He needs to quit underrating himself. He needs continually to remind himself of Jesus' expectation of him:

". . . The works that I do shall he do also; and greater works than these shall he do. . ."

END OF THE WORLD

"EVERYTHING IS GOING TO BE ALL RIGHT," the woman said tearfully as I tried to console her.

She had a few days before received news that brought a shocking disappointment to her. Her husband had an incurable disease. I wondered if she would bear up under the blow.

Then she added: "You know, not too long ago I had another bitter disappointment. Our doctor then told us one of our children had a critically serious disease. At the time, I thought the world was coming to an end for us. But somehow things have worked out. They will again."

As we continued to talk, I concluded that this good woman had come to accept disappointment with courage.

A Scottish barrister with a golden pen — Sir Walter Scott — seemd to have learned to receive disappointment even as a friend. Before he was two, Scott was stricken with a severe illness which left him lame. This must have been a distressing disappointment to the tot's parents.

But for the boy Walter, his lameness helped lead him

————————

January, 1962.

into a wonderful new world of story telling. He could not play like other boys. His parents sent him to his grandfather's farm to regain his strength. There, day after day, he listened wide-eyed to stories his aunt read to him.

From that start, Scott became an international hero as a narrative poet. For years his name glittered in the glory of fame.

Then, the brilliant works of another poet, Byron, began winning the public's favor.

But Byron's popularity was not the "end of the world" for Scott. If it was a disappointment, Scott accepted it as a friend. He turned his pen to prose. And it was his resulting historical novels — *Ivanhoe*, *The Talisman*, and others — which won him his crowning place in literature.

There is a teen-age girl [1] in our area who has undergone surgery 17 times. One of her operations, when she was nine, was on her hands, stiffened by a rare disease. After surgery, the physician told her mother: "Keep her fingers moving." She did, with the piano. At 17 the girl had given her first public concert.

A construction worker I met received disappointment in a crippling injury. He turned to accounting, opening before him a new world of business. There is a woman [2] who, with one child and another yet to be born, lost her husband. Disappointment became discovery for the new widow. Through struggle and faith, she earned a doctorate and became head of a university department of home economics. This led to world travel to teach others.

----

[1] Ruth Romney.
[2] Dr. Virginia F. Cutler.

Then there was a World War II marine from Wyoming.[3] On this particular morning he was going ashore in the invasion of Peleliu, a tiny Pacific coral isle. The enemy was ready, in Bloody Nose Ridge caves. The zero moment neared when some men prayed, silently, perhaps, or in low tones, but fervently. But this marine "couldn't get in the spirit of it." He explained: "I was taught in chemistry class that nothing was so unless you could prove it, and I had no way of proving God."

On the fifteenth day after invasion, as the Wyoming marine spliced a broken telephone wire, he was struck in the leg by a sniper's bullet. Six days later, on a hospital ship he was told that the leg would be amputated next day. The wounded man asked if there were any other Mormons aboard. Two were found, and together the three prayed. On the morrow the leg came off — no doubt a painful disappointment to the marine.

Approximately a year later, he rose to his feet, one of them of wood, in the mission home. "On that hospital ship," he said, "I lost my leg, but I found God."

This is a time of the year to count blessings. Perhaps as you count yours, you may wish to name those which began with a disappointment. The number may surprise you. You may even discover that what at the time seemed like "the end of the world" actually was instead a key — to an exciting new world of achievement and happiness and faith.

---

[3] Cornelius (Neil) Workman.

MAGINOT LINES

They laid him away the other day. At his passing he was all but forgotten. He was a comparatively young man.

I remember him 30 years ago. He was a hero then. In our world of sport, he was a king. He was tall and dark and handsome, too. Wise men of sport talked glowingly of his future as a professional.

But he captured few headlines as a pro. Reasons were given. Among them was the one that the fellow had too much ability and good looks for his own good. Others with less ability passed him by. They bore down while he played.

His strength seemed to be the cause of his weakness.

The lowly tentmaker of Tarsus who became the mighty Apostle Paul once wrote: ". . . when I am weak, then am I strong." [1] Some men become strong through weakness. Others become weak through strength.

I shall never forget Europe in 1936. Hitler's legions were goose stepping. Throughout Germany, we found the atmosphere electric — like a college campus on the

---

September, 1960.

[1] *II Corinthians* 12:10.

eve of a big game. Helmeted men paraded, tanks rolled, bombers maneuvered through the sky.

Yet, in France we found the atmosphere quite different. Artists with palettes lined the Seine in Paris. Covers on magazine racks portrayed styles and pretty women. People in France and the other western countries did not seem to worry too much. After all, between France and Hitler's goose stepping Germany was the mighty Maginot Line.

No enemy army could cross that Maginot Line. Of rock-like concrete and steeel, it had been constructed after World War I to prevent another German invasion of the West. The Maginot Line was 250 miles long. Above ground, it was a deep line of bristling forts, flanked by pillboxes and barbed wire entanglements. Below were chambers for housing great numbers of soldiers. And there were vast underground storehouses, hospitals, garages and communication systems.

"Let Hitler shout about war," people said. "The Allies have the Maginot Line."

In 1939, Hitler's armored divisions crashed into Poland. It was a quick, smashing victory. That was to the east. The West still had its Maginot Line.

Then on a May dawn less than a year later the skies reddened over Holland, Belgium and northern France. Swarms of Nazi bombers had begun the attack. In little over a month Paris had surrendered. Then Hitler's armies moved toward the Maginot Line from the rear. It was taken easily. France was crushed.

The Allies, it seemed, had become weak through the strength of their Maginot Line.

Every man has his strengths. Some build on them.

Others lean on them, and they become their undoing. They become "Maginot Lines."

I knew a man who seemed to be forever telling others of the achievements of his noble father. As he talked, the man's own stature seemed to fade. He let his father's greatness become his own weakness.

There was another man. He was born with a golden tongue. Smooth words tumbled from it effortlessly. But the man seemed to give little time to his talks. Often he spoke too long. People wearied in his words. A strength became his weakness. Other men similarly have let other abilities, money or a talented, toiling wife become their "Maginot Lines."

Then there is a leader I heard speak this week. His voice is like an organ. He is handsome, poised and polished. He held an audience of some six thousand spellbound. As I listened I could count hours of hard sweat behind his thrilling message. In it were many lines that only long labor could unleash. On his strength the man [2] had built greater strength.

Four well-known words in the Bible represent a long, thrilling story of building greater strength on strength — of sons building on the greatness of their fathers and on their own strengths as well. The words are names: Abraham, Isaac, Jacob and Joseph. Each built a greater fortress of character on his own "Maginot Line."

_____

[2] Hugh B. Brown.

DUMPING SLAG

It looked at night like a huge bolt of bright orange ribbon rolling down the hillside, leaving a glowing trail behind.

It was the dumping of the hot slag from the smelter. I remember vividly that repeated sight from my boyhood. We used to watch it from our broad, wooden front porch. The slag was dumped near the lake and mountain to the west of our valley where, shortly before, a flaming sunset had often faded into a darkening sky.

Then I remember our trips to swim in the salty lake. We passed the slag dump on the way. There it was — that black, lifeless heap of smelter waste. It was a depressing sight.

Those memories came spinning back across my mind the other night when I turned the page in a national news magazine. My eyes stopped on a beautiful, full-page color advertisement portraying a fleet of sailboats and closeups of large, plump oysters. The advertisement was headlined:

"They grow to luscious size in 'nurseries' of steel plant slag." [1]

―――――――

December, 1959.

[1] *Time*, September 14, 1959, page 117.

The advertisement then told how 20,000 tons of slag were sowed overboard last summer at several locations in Chesapeake Bay.

And that was the beginning of an exciting new chapter in the life of that once dull, black ore waste.

After the slag had been poured onto the ocean floor, things began to happen. There were millions of oyster eggs in the area, and in a mass they looked like thick cream. Hatched, a new little oyster is cupshaped and about the size of a pin point. The infant oyster has a tiny foot which is used as a feeler to select a place on which to cling. For about two weeks these baby oysters swim around in search of a home. The decision is important, because once an attachment is made, it is permanent.

Oyster after oyster selected the bed of slag. Soon there was a large mass of robustly growing young oysters attached to the slag. There, feeding on myriad ocean plant and animal organisms, they grew to luscious size.

Men, like slag, so often decline into dullness as they withdraw to themselves with the lengthening years. But life so many times becomes more exciting, and men's statures grow, as they mingle with youth. Particularly is this so when a man helps youth to a point where they really attach themselves to him — like young oysters clinging to slag on the ocean floor.

This week I have been dipping into the days of three of the world's great minds. All lived in ancient Greece. First was a bald, ugly man with a flat nose and thick lips, who wandered like a beggar through Athens' streets. But centuries later, Milton called him "wisest of men." His name was Socrates. His deep thought on morality moved men for generations. It has been said that his chief work was with youth. And no doubt Socrates was taller in stature because younger men, like Plato, followed him — followed him even to the scene of his death in a prison cell where he had been ordered to drink poison.

Plato, 43 years younger than Socrates, was 43 years older than Aristotle. For 20 years, until the death of Plato, young Aristotle was his student. Plato doubtless was stimulated to greater achievement by Aristotle's attachment, even as Socrates had been motivated by young Plato.

As you follow the life of handsome, refined and gentle Aristotle you find him repeatedly seeking youth to teach. He was tutor in the Macedonian court. Later, he opened a school in the Athens area — in the covered portico of a gymnasium. It was known as the Lyceum. There he taught for years.

Among those Aristotle tutored was a bright, strong-willed boy who became Alexander the Great. Surely Aristotle was greater because of his association with youth such as Alexander the Great!

It has been said that a man stands tallest when he stoops for a child. That is what the story of the slag and the oysters seems to say — as well as the lives of the three great Greeks: Socrates, Plato, and Aristotle.

"WHAT NEXT?"

IT HAS BEEN ALMOST TEN YEARS since my silver-haired friend said he was going to retire in just a few years. But he is still very much on the job. He is vigorously directing a growing business and doing his full share of community building. He never seemed happier.

My friend has not told me so, but he has probably made up his mind that the truly happy man never retires. His work may change, but he keeps forever at it.

Take the case of the late Sir Malcolm Campbell.

I have seen a speed car move like a meteor across the glistening Bonneville salt flats. But I was not there when Sir Malcolm, with his *Bluebird,* in 1935 set a world speed mark. I was a missionary in his England at the time, and recall the excitement his victory caused in London.

With Sir Malcolm on the salt flats was his son Donald. Twenty years later, Donald set a world water speed record. He did it with a jet-propelled speedboat, *Bluebird,* on glassy smooth Ullswater, an English lake. He had won back from America the water speed record his late father had once held.

—————————

January, 1960.

one hundred twenty-three

After the run, a reporter pushed through the cheering crowd. He asked Donald Campbell: "What next?" The speedster could not answer. In his hotel room later he still had no answer. He could remember an accident four years before in which he had miraculously escaped death. At 170 miles per hour, his speedboat had crashed into a submerged railway tie. He recalled too, that other men had died attempting the speed he had just reached.

Then Donald Campbell remembered a letter from his father 23 years before. Donald at the time was in preparatory school. He wanted to be the school's best rifleman. He had proudly written his father about his practice score of 205 out of 210. Donald told his father he would shoot for another 205 in the big test, and should easily win the title. His father wrote back: "You've already been there. Shoot for 210." He counseled his son to never rest on his honors. If he achieved one goal, he should set another.

Donald shot for 210. He scored 208, setting a school record that stood 27 years later.

Donald also remembered the days after his father had set the world land speed record of 301 miles per hour on the salt flats in 1935. The elder Campbell had promised his family he would retire after reaching the 300 mark.

But in retirement, Sir Malcolm's life lost its zest. There was no challenge. Donald reminded him that he had attained his goal but had not set another one. Sir Malcolm then decided to seek also the world water speed record. He won it on Lake Maggiore in the Italian Alps two years later.

World War II came, and Sir Malcolm as an officer carefully observed jet fighter planes. He wondered if jet propulsion could be used with boats. After the war, he began to tackle his new challenge, but a heart attack took him before he had finished.

Now Donald announced a new goal: to reach 300 m.p.h. on water and 400 m.p.h. on land — with jet power.[1]

The Campbells have dramatically demonstrated what a noted physician counseled in our city recently: "Don't retire from life or life will retire from you." [2]

Another great name in sports when I was a young reporter was Amos Alonzo Stagg. An All-American in football at Yale, he coached at the University of Chicago for 41 years. His teams won 254 games, lost 104, and tied 28. At 71, he was retired by Chicago. But he did not retire. He began anew, as coach at the College of the Pacific in Stockton, California. Ten years later he was voted America's "coach of the year." Later, Pacific retired him. He joined his son as co-coach at Susquehanna University in Pennsylvania. At 89 Stagg saw his team there finish the season without a loss or tie — for the first time in the school's history. As he approached the century mark, grand old Amos Alonzo Stagg seemed to be still setting new goals for himself.

After a nerve-knocking day at the office, I often am tempted to thoughts of future retirement. In those hours I hope the names of the Campbells and Stagg will loom up. I hope I will then ask myself the reporter's question:

---

[1] Campbell, Donald, "The Best Advice I Ever Had," *Reader's Digest*, August, 1959, pages 107-110.
[2] Dr. Edward L. Bortz, former president American Medical Association, as reported by William C. Patrick, *The Salt Lake Tribune*, Sept. 17, 1959.

"What next?"

Surely, genuine joy comes not through letup. Rather, it comes through new challenges, through continuing progress — into eternity.

CHRISTMAS TREE COUNTRY

ONCE A YEAR OUR FAMILY MANAGES to get together for a shopping trip. It is to buy a Christmas tree. All must have a voice in this purchase.

Chances are this year's tree will be a Douglas fir from northwestern Montana. First, because Montana firs are yule favorites across America. Secondly, our vacation last summer was spent in the heart of Montana's Christmas tree country.

A Montana tree will remind us of what we learned about that state's firs — why they make superior Christmas ornaments.

The growing season in Kootenai Forest is short, so the trees do not develop too fast. The limbs, as a result, grow closer together; and the foliage is thicker and heavier. Because these Montana trees become dormant in the cold weather before the cutting season, they hold their foliage longer. They do not shed their needles so soon.

Yes, a Montana tree will bring back many vivid summer memories — of battling silvery landlocked salmon; of swimming in glacier-fed, fir-fringed Flathead Lake; and of strolls into the timbered hills, scented with wild clover and sweet peas and mountain roses.

————————

December, 1961.

But perhaps more than all these, our Christmas tree this year will remind us of a couple we met in that verdantly rugged country last summer. They are the Kolbys, Bess and Am. They operate the lodgings on Flathead Lake where we stayed.

When Bess Kolby met us, we saw a smiling, sun-browned face. It bore the lines of toil. Hers was a pointed chin that showed resolute determination. Her dark brown eyes measured fast. Her spare frame moved briskly.

She showed us to our unit with knotty pine walls. It was nothing fancy, but it was clean as a clinic. "Just a minute," she said. "This place will not be ready until I put something on that table." From her garden she brought a bouquet of peonies, daisies, and a tall pinkish purple flower whose bloom was shaped like a lodgepole pine. (We later learned its name: blue pine.)

We did not expect a bouquet like this. But it turned out to be one of many quiet little kindnesses the Kolbys surprised us with during our week's stay.

Am Kolby is tall, fortyish, and soft-spoken. He always wore khaki, with a blue, visored fisherman's cap, and faded blue canvas shoes. He wore horn-rimmed glasses and there was always a glove on one artificial hand. Am guided us to lake waters where salmon tugged often on our lines. After we had cleaned our catch, he took us to his outdoor cupboard. "Here, try this for cooking your fish," he said. He handed me a 14-inch heavy iron griddle. Then he took me to an outdoor stove and showed me how to make a good cooking fire.

Next morning, as I prepared to cook the fish, I found a lusty fire already blazing in the outdoor stove. Am Kolby had quietly begun his good turns early!

The extra courtesies continued through the week — from taking our 9-year-old son for a ride in his three-wheel electric car to surprising us with a huge outdoor fire and marshmallow sticks on a chilly night.

Nor were all the Kolbys' kindnesses directed to people. Only a few days before we arrived, one of their ducks had been attacked by a mink. The duck had survived but showed a deep wound in its neck. The duck was given first aid and later taken to a veterinary, for a fee larger than a duck is worth — to most everyone but the Kolbys. During our stay we watched the patient, spoonfeeding care that duck received — from a busy couple, busy with the day's tasks and with quiet kindnesses to others.

So as we purchase our tree this year, our thoughts will turn to Montana's tall timber country and to those lives which stand so tall in our memories. Yes, the Kolbys brought the spirit of Christmas to us in June and reminded us again of the words of Him whose birth those yule firs honor:

"'But when thou doest alms, let not thy left hand know what thy right hand doeth:

"That thine alms may be in secret: and thy Father which seeth in secret himself shall reward thee openly." [1]

--- --- --- ---

[1] *Matthew* 6:3, 4.

WITH WINGS OR ON FOOT

A SHORT TIME AGO I CALLED AT THE OFFICE of a friend [1] who is president of a financial institution in our city. It was midmorning, and I found furniture in his office stacked and covered with canvas. The gold-colored carpet was soaking wet. My friend, wearing a heavy sports coat, sat chatting with an associate in the lobby. There were no lights.

Sawdust was strewn around the floor. The telephones were not working. There was no heat nor air conditioning. There were damp spots in the ceiling. Employes were scurrying about, or talking in small knots.

The night before there had been a spectacular fire on the top floor of the historic downtown building which houses the business. Firemen's water had seeped down into the floors below. My friend's place was a sorry sight that morning.

But the president was cheerful and calm. He was busy making plans to replace the soaked carpet, remove water stains, and get the electricity operating.

It was not long before business was being transacted.

The following day, I broke a large circular glass covering for the lighting fixture in our dining room while

August, 1963.
[1] M. L. Dye.

trying to adjust it. My first impulse was to let the broken lighting fixture go for a few days. Then it would not seem so suddenly expensive to replace the glass.

But I thought of my friend after the fire. He had wasted no time by harboring his misfortune. I went directly to the electric shop. The mishap would soon be forgotten.

An old proverb says: "Misfortunes come on wings and depart on foot." [2] Perhaps most of our misfortunes depart on foot because we harbor them. We allow them to linger. I can remember broken windows I have let linger even though there was insurance to cover. There were dents in car fenders, too; and untended nicks in the furniture and spots on the rug. As I have let them linger, they have kept reminding me of the incidents which brought them. The misfortunes have departed on a heavy foot.

But broken windows and carpet spots are small things. There are scars of larger misfortunes — times we were passed by without promotions, defeated for office, disappointed in love, laid low by poor health or injury, crushed by a friend's blow, or let down by a kinsman's folly. It is so easy to harbor setbacks like those, to let the cracks in our feelings linger. If we let them remain long enough they become open breaks. And through them ill winds often blow in upon our souls.

One of the touching love stories of the scriptures is that of Jacob and Rachel. They first met at the well of Haran. Rachel was tending her father's sheep. Jacob rolled the stone from the well's mouth, and watered the

---

[2] Bohn, Henry G., *A Hand-Book of Proverbs*, London, England, George Bell & Sons, 1889 edition, page 452.

sheep. Rachel was a beautiful girl and of Jacob's people. He kissed her and wept. Then he agreed to serve Rachel's father Laban seven years for her hand. The years ". . . seemed unto him but a few days, for the love he had to her." [3]

Then misfortune struck Jacob. For his seven years' toil Rachel's father gave Jacob her elder sister Leah instead of Rachel. It must have been a jolting blow to Jacob. It could have driven him away with bitterness or despair. But *Genesis* says only that he toiled seven more years for Laban.

Jacob no doubt found that after a reverse it is more blessed to drip with sweat than tears. Work for him apparently gave wings to misfortune. In the end he won Rachel; and she became the mother of Joseph, one of the noblemen of all history.

Perhaps there is no real disaster in any of our lives. To all of us there come misfortunes. They seem disastrous only when we let them linger and make them depart with heavy foot.

That was what my business friend's actions told me that morning after the fire. That is what Jacob's toil for Laban tells.

With love in his heart, forgiveness in his soul, and sweat on his brow, Jacob apparently gave to his misfortune not only wings; he gave to it a happy ending.

---

[3] *Genesis* 29:20.

BY THE GOLDEN GATE

TOMORROW IS COMING TOO SOON. Tomorrow brings to an end this week in San Francisco.

I have been in San Francisco many times, and each visit seems to be more exciting than the last.

I love San Francisco. I like its hills. I always seem to be moving upward in San Francisco. I like its jerking, clanging cable cars. They make me feel young again — like riding a rocking horse. San Francisco always has flowers in her hand — gay hues in carnations, daisies, roses, and chrysanthemums in the downtown stalls.

I like San Francisco's food: the fresh, tender crab at Fisherman's Wharf, the Italian soup at Alfred's and roasted peking duck at Kan's. I like the tangy, sea-rinsed air, and the city's homes and buildings which stand so close and tall, always as if at attention. I like the way the city's people move — spiritedly but not hurriedly. They seem to know where they are going.

I like the Golden Gate Park with its own Cedars of Lebanon, its banks of rhododendrons, its beds of dahlias, and its Japanese gardens with swan-rippled ponds and Portals of the Past. Most of all, though I like the

---

February, 1964.

one hundred thirty-three

park for its broad lawns which beckon youth to play.

But this week I think I discovered why I really love San Francisco.

It was early Tuesday morning. We had been out to dinner the night before and noticed that our 13-year-old, Marged, wore a coat that needed cleaning.

Through a light drizzle I took the dark-blue coat to a little, narrow-fronted cleaning shop on Sutter Street.

As I handed the coat to the lone Chinese man in the place, he looked at the coat, the drizzle outside, and then at me. I was a stranger. Yet he seemed to hardly want to accept the coat.

"She will need this coat today," he said.

"We'll manage," I replied. "How soon may I have it?"

"I'll get it ready by three o'clock," he promised.

That afternoon Marged called for her coat. It was raining again. Her coat was ready all right. As the Chinese cleaning man, thirtyish and rather short, took the coat from the rack, he removed the plastic covering. "Will you wait a minute?" he asked, kindly. His deft fingers began fashioning the plastic into a rain bonnet.

Finished, the Chinese gentleman passed his handiwork to Marged and smiled, "There!"

Happily she moved out into the rain.

San Francisco is big and powerful and pretentious as cities of the world go, all right. But she is not too mighty nor too busy to proudly claim a string of little shops — corner groceries, laundries, and cleaners — around her pretty peninsular neck.

San Francisco, among the family of great cities, stands tall because she has a heart. Even to a stranger she stands tall because she strives to be warm and human and tender — like the Chinese man I met on Sutter Street.

That, I guess, is why I really love the city by the Golden Gate.

HERO WHERE HE LOST

AMONG THE CITIES OF NORTH AMERICA it is a Methuselah that is different.

Quebec, rising like a fortress on the high cliffs over the silver-gray St. Lawrence River, is old. The city was founded in 1608 by a handsome French explorer, Samuel de Champlain.

We found towered, turreted Quebec full of Old World charm. We wound through narrow, hilly streets where hoofbeats still sound. We munched bread browned to chewy goodness in a wood-burning, outdoor, brick oven on the outskirts of town.

Like most cities, Quebec has its heroes. But Quebec's real hero, if you consider places and buildings named for the man, is the eighteenth century French soldier, Marquis de Montcalm.[1] There are Montcalm Hotel, Montcalm Square, and Palais Montcalm — the city's civic center. A 220-acre National Battlefields Park has been dedicated where Montcalm rode to battle in defense of Quebec. A large, stone monument honors him and his opposing general, James Wolfe.

Why does this old French city so honor Montcalm? After all, he was the Frenchman who lost the city to

October, 1964.
[1] Montcalm de Saint-Veran, de (Marquis Louis Joseph).

the British on that September day in 1759. More than that, Montcalm's crushing defeat before Wolfe lost for France her vast empire in the New World.

Several times we walked across those rolling Plains of Abraham where Montcalm's army was routed by Wolfe's.

Young gangling James Wolfe's troops at 4 a.m. on September 13, 1759, had moved ashore at a cove about two miles west of Quebec. They clambered up the cliff and four hours later were poised on the Plains for battle.

Riding a black charger, Montcalm led his white-uniformed French army across the Plains to meet the scarlet lines of the British.

Montcalm had much to make his heart heavy on that eventful morning. Eight days before he had placed a French regiment to guard the very cove where Wolfe had landed. Two days later, the vain, temperamental governor of Canada, Vendreuil, had ordered the regiment away from the cove. This was only one of many instances where the governor had crossed the general.

But that morning against Wolfe found Montcalm riding in front of his lines giving encouragement to some 5,000 men. When he ordered an advance, the army moved in three columns, with Montcalm leading the center. Meanwhile, Wolfe had commanded his troops to hold their fire until the enemy was 40 paces away. During the brief battle, Wolfe was mortally wounded in the chest and died as his army pursued the French toward Quebec. Montcalm was struck in the stomach and thigh. When he was told he had only a few hours to live, he said: "So much the better, as I shall not live long enough to see the surrender of Quebec." He died the next day.[2]

Montcalm was gallant in death as he had been through a life of 47 years. As a youth he had written his life's aims to his father. Young Montcalm began: "1. To be an honorable man of good morals, brave and a Christian." He also expressed a desire for learning and "intellectual accuracy," to honor his parents, and "fence and ride as well as my small abilities will permit."[3]

That seemed to be Montcalm's lifelong code. As a French soldier in his teens, he used the long leisure hours to learn German and Greek. At 40, he wrote of his children (the Montcalms were to have ten): "May the world preserve them all and make them prosper for this world and the next."[4]

Before meeting Wolfe, Montcalm scored brilliant victories in the New World, at Fort Oswego and Fort William Henry. At Ticonderoga, with 3,800 men he repulsed a British force of 15,000.

After Montcalm fell on the Plains of Abraham, one of his officers wrote: 'I can never console myself for the loss of my general. . . . He was a good general, a zealous citizen, a reliable friend, and a father of us all."[5]

Montcalm lost Quebec, but he won the esteem of its citizens through many generations. He won because he seemed to stay true to his boyhood desire of living nobly and fighting gallantly. That is what I hope to remember from a visit to quaint Quebec.

---

[2] Samuel, Sigmund, *The Seven Years War in Canada*, Toronto, Canada, The Tyerson Press, 1934, page 110.
[3] Doughty, A. and G. W. Parmelee, *The Siege of Quebec and the Battle of the Plains of Abraham*, Volume 1, Quebec, Canada, Dassault & Proulx, 1901, page 1932.
[4] *The Siege of Quebec and the Battle of the Plains of Abraham*, pages 133, 134.
[5] *The Siege of Quebec and the Battle of the Plains of Abraham*, Volume 3, page 169.

BOOK FIVE

Be Of Good Courage

"Wait on the Lord;
be of good courage,
and he shall strengthen
thine heart."
   —Psalms 27:14

DAVID'S FINEST HOUR

OUR 10-YEAR-OLD SON, OWEN, had an assignment to tell the story of David and Goliath. I volunteered to help him.

We turned to the 17th chapter of *I Samuel.* Our story began in a valley called Elah. The Philistines stood on the slopes of one mountain. Across the valley, on another mountainside, were the armies of Israel.

From out of the Philistine camp strode into the valley their champion: Goliath of Gath. Samuel says he was six cubits and a span tall.

"How big is that?" Owen wondered. We probed. A cubit was the distance from the tip of the middle finger to the elbow — 18 to 21 inches. That would make Goliath about ten feet tall.

Samuel says Goliath wore a helmet of brass. He also wore a coat of mail. The coat was as heavy as 5,000 shekels of brass. How heavy was that? A shekel was about half an ounce. We figured with a pencil.

"That would make the weight of his coat 160 pounds," I said.

Goliath was big. He was also strong.

Goliath was well protected. He also wore armor of

———————

November, 1962.

brass over his legs, from his feet to his knees. Besides his coat of mail, he wore a "target of brass between his shoulders." [1] A target was a small shield. In addition to all this, "one bearing a shield went before him." [2]

Goliath carried a mighty spear. Samuel describes its iron head as weighing 600 shekels. "That is nearly 20 pounds, as heavy as this portable typewriter," I explained to Owen. He hefted the typewriter. "That's plenty heavy," he agreed.

Every morning and evening for 40 days Goliath bellowed his challenge.

Three eldest of the eight sons of Jesse were with Israel's army. Jesse's youngest son, David, watched his father's sheep at Bethlehem. He was a handsome lad, with ruddy face. He, as a harpist, had previously delighted Israel's king, Saul.

Now Jesse asked David to take food to his soldier brothers: a bushel of parched corn and ten loaves. David was also to take ten cheeses to his brothers' captain.

David found his brothers entrenched for battle. As he chatted with them Goliath came out with his challenge. David saw the warriors of Israel flee in fright before him.

Owen and I read on.

But mighty Goliath held no terror for David. "Who is this . . . Philistine, that he should defy the armies of the living God?" [3] David asked. He would meet Goliath.

----

[1] *I Samuel* 17:6.
[2] *I Samuel* 17:7.
[3] *I Samuel* 17:26.

David's eldest brother Eliab was upset. He inquired why David had come to the battlefield. Eliab also wanted to know who was looking after the sheep.

But David's words reached King Saul. He called for the young harpist. Saul reminded David that he would be a youth against a seasoned man of war.

David was unshaken. The Lord had helped him, while with the sheep, conquer a lion and a bear. "He will deliver me out of the hand of this Philistine," [4] David assured the king. There was a vibrant vigor about his faith, something fresh that had come down from out of Bethlehem's hills.

David put off the armor Saul offered him. The lad went to a brook. He selected five smooth stones. With them in his shepherd's bag and a sling in his hand, David moved into the valley to meet Goliath.

The giant growled: "Am I a dog?" [5] Then Goliath told David how he would destroy him and feed his flesh to the fowls of the air and the beasts of the field.

David was not impressed. After all, Goliath was only a man. "This day will the Lord deliver thee into mine hand," [6] he answered.

And David, with God's help, conquered.

There it was: the thrilling story I have read and re-read many times. But moving through it with Owen gave me a new appreciation of David in the valley of Elah. His faith had new vigor for a boy looking ahead at life, and a man looking ahead at problems. It was a faith I hope my son can acquire and keep — and his son and his son's son, too!

---

[4] *I Samuel* 17:37.
[5] *I Samuel* 17:43.
[6] *I Samuel* 17:46.

REBEL IN LONDON

IT WAS A BRIGHT SPRING DAY IN LONDON, and the city's blossoming parks were beginning to look as though it had been snowing pink. Our big, double-deck red bus had just passed over the Thames River near the Houses of Parliament. Now in Trafalgar Square we had paused to transfer to another bus.

Behind us was the National Portrait Gallery, containing hundreds of portraits, some in marble and bronze, of Britain's great. Before us, rising like a giant needle in the center of the Square, was Nelson's Monument. Tall as a twenty-story building, its granite shaft was topped by a 14-foot statue of the national hero, Lord Nelson.

To tradition-loving Britons, Trafalgar was heroes' square all right.

As we waited for our bus, in a garden fronting the National Portrait Gallery, our eyes stopped on a life-size statue of George Washington.

It is 26 years now since I stood before that statue at Trafalgar Square in London. But the lesson lingers on. Some 30 years before Lord Nelson's triumph at Trafalgar in 1805, George Washington and other American

------

June, 1962.

colonists started a war against Mother Britain. He was
a rebel. England sent the largest expeditionary force in
its history to put him down. Even after Trafalgar,
Washington remained a scoundrel to Britons. During
the War of 1812, Robert Southey, Britain's poet laureate,
wrote:

> "The indignant land,
> Where Washington hath left,
> His awful memory. . ." [1]

Now, we stood before a monument to that rebel
American in heroes' square in London.

No people anywhere have greater stature in character
than the sons of Britain. Perhaps one of the reasons is
that they have been willing to admit they have been
wrong at times. That statue on Trafalgar Square of
America's Revolutionary leader seemed to say: We
could have been wrong about George Washington.

It is a big man who will voluntarily admit he has
erred.

Years ago, I had a little "Battle of Trafalgar" with a
business friend. The atmosphere blued as words were
hurled. I was probably as much at fault as he. But, a
few days later, a hand-penned letter arrived on my desk.
My opponent wrote that he had been wrong. He was
older and higher on the business ladder than I. His letter
took great courage. My bitterness turned to esteem.
Today he tours the globe as a top executive of a world-
wide business.

No doubt much of the great respect accorded George
Washington came from his willingness to admit a

––––––––––
[1] *Ode,* written in 1814.

mistake. Francis Rufus Bellamy [2] tells an experience of Washington at 17, when he was a frontier surveyor. A political contest was on, and an argument developed between young Washington and an older man. Washington had a violent temper. It burst into a searing volley of words. With this, the man, a Mr. Payne, struck young George with a stick, hard enough to knock the tall youth to the ground.

Washington later wrote a note to Mr. Payne, asking to meet him next morning in the local tavern, to discuss their disagreements. Payne was there, expecting more trouble from the young hothead. When they met, George acknowledged his mistake, and asked for forgiveness for what he had done in an unguarded moment.

Jesus reserved one of his greatest tributes for another soldier, a man He apparently never met—a Roman centurion. The centurion sent friends to ask the Master to heal a servant. The Roman explained that he himself was not worthy to come to Jesus. The officer also discouraged Jesus from entering his home ". . . for I am not worthy that thou shouldest enter under my roof." The Roman added: ". . . but say in a word, and my servant shall be healed." [3]

What made the centurion's great faith really glisten was his admission of his unworthiness, in his own eyes at least, to meet the Master.

The words "I was wrong" in the twinkling of a tongue can turn anger into admiration. In seconds they can unravel yards of complications between people

_____

[2] Bellamy, Francis Rufus, *The Private Life of George Washington*, New York, N. Y., Thomas Y. Crowell Company, 1951.
[3] *Luke* 7:6-7.

over the back fence, on the job, or almost anywhere. Those words help a man become bigger than himself.

That is the lesson that lingers from the statue of Washington in Trafalgar Square.

SECOND CHANCE

THERE IS NOTHING QUITE LIKE a morning stroll through the French quarter in old New Orleans. The small-paned windows and the green shutters on the little two-story brick homes seem to whisper of the gay past. So do the countless balconies, decorated elegantly with lacework in iron.

As we walked and rode through this storied old city, there kept coming up a name that charmed us. It was Jean Lafitte. New Orleans people stopped and looked when he walked these same streets shortly after the city came under the Stars and Stripes in 1803. Some called him a pirate; others, a polished gentleman. Some said he was a bandit. He was called a Robin Hood, too. Many count him among America's real heroes in war.

Jean Lafitte probably wore all those hats — and many more.

But as I have dug into his record, there comes out of it a story that men everywhere could well remember.[1]

One November day in 1813, there was posted in New Orleans a notice from the first governor of Louisiana. A reward of $500 was offered anyone who would deliver Jean Lafitte to the sheriff.

May, 1961.
[1] See Arthur, Stanley Clisby, *Jean Lafitte, Gentleman Lover,* New Orleans, Louisiana, Harmanson, publisher, 1952 edition.

Lafitte and his several hundred men styled themselves as privateers. The fine silks, velvets, jewels and other prizes they took at sea were brought to Lafitte's hideout, Grande Isle, a short distance south of New Orleans. Then they were sold to the city's elite.

Governor Claiborne's notice amused tall, black-haired, trim-bearded Jean Lafitte. A few days later, Lafitte posted a notice of his own. He offered an even larger reward to anyone who would deliver Governor Claiborne to him.

New Orleans people really chuckled — and Jean Lafitte continued his traffic in smuggled goods.

Then one September day in 1814, a British warship appeared offshore from Lafitte's rendezvous. Three officers brought to him a message from the commander of His Majesty's forces in the Floridas. Britain was at war with America and planned a major attack on New Orleans. The commander asked Lafitte and his men to join the British. The reward: a captaincy for Lafitte, free lands after victory for his men, freedom for Lafitte's brother-partner now in irons in a New Orleans jail for smuggling, and a cash bonus of $30,000 for Lafitte.

Lafitte requested a fortnight to make his decision.

He then sent the British document to Governor Claiborne, at the same time volunteering his services to the American cause. All he asked was a pardon. "I am a stray sheep wishing to return to the flock," he wrote.

Governor Claiborne called a meeting of American military leaders in Louisiana. They voted, Claiborne abstaining, to move against Lafitte and his men with United States warships.

Lafitte offered no resistance but slipped away to a

friend's plantation on the Mississippi. He still asked to fight for his adopted country.

Meanwhile, rough, red-haired Andrew Jackson was called to lead the American forces in the battle which Lafitte had warned was coming. Pleas were made to Jackson to let Lafitte and his men join the colors. Jackson roared, "No!" They were pirates and robbers.

After the British had captured American gunboats near New Orleans, Governor Claiborne appealed to Jackson to permit Lafitte to join up. "Old Hickory" growled something, and the Governor took it as an approval. He issued an order inviting Lafitte and his men to fight with the United States.

A few days later — on January 8, 1815 — some 14,000 Wellington-trained redcoats moved against the Americans. Jackson had 3,700 sharpshooters, including Lafitte's "rowdies," waited for them behind cotton bales. Lafitte himself, on one of his boats, helped protect the water flank of the battle.

The British were routed, leaving hundreds of casualties on the field. The American dead: 13.

In our New Orleans tour, we paused at that battlefield. It is one to remember. There, victory came, in a large measure, because Louisiana's first governor gave another chance to a "stray sheep." The governor gave a second chance to Jean Lafitte, the colorful smuggler who had once publicly belittled the man who now forgave him.

RIDE TO FREEDOM

SINCE THE DEAR, DEAD DAYS ALMOST BEYOND RECALL, I have had what I thought was a vivid picture of that most famous of American rides. Young Paul Revere jumped as if aroused by a pistol shot onto his spirited mount. Then for a good part of the night he rode like lightning. He raced down one colonial lane after another, his steed steaming under his pressing spurs. Breathlessly he would tell a nightshirted farmer the redcoats were coming, and gallop onto the next.

Then I got into the account of Revere's ride by an able biographer, Esther Forbes. She details it in her 510-page volume, *Paul Revere and the World He Lived In.*[1] Briefly, this is the picture which emerges from her book:

Paul Revere was 40 when he made the ride. His was a stocky build, with thick neck, brown eyes, brown hair and a wide mouth. He was the personification of steadiness. He looked like a man who would remain calm when his house was aflame. He was known for his deft work with his hands: elegant silver, fine copper engravings and hand-carved false teeth.

Paul Revere did not jump onto *his* own horse on that

July, 1960.
[1] Published in 1942 by Houghton Mifflin Company, Boston, Massachusetts.

historic April night in 1775. The animal was a friend's. It was the best in the stable of one of the wealthiest citizens of Charlestown, the Boston suburb where Revere began his ride. The horse was slender, rather small and nervous. But it was surefooted and tireless.

Author Forbes notes that Revere did not mount in a scramble. There was time to get the "feel" of his animal — and to test the stirrups for length and the girths for firmness. He began his ride at 11 p.m.

Paul Revere, his biographer makes clear, rode with care. He knew that there were redcoats hiding in the leafing bushes along the way — to intercept Yankee messengers. His horse must have enough reserve for that extra spurt of speed when so challenged by the lurking enemy.

That Revere rode with care is attested by the excellent condition of his mount immediately after the five-hour mission.

As Paul had almost crossed Charlestown Common, he noticed two British officers on horseback ahead. They waited under a tree where the road narrowed. One started his horse toward the American. Revere's steed had the required reserve. In a brief, slippery race, his light-footed horse outran the heavier British charger. Paul Revere rode on to alarm the Minute Men along the trail to Lexington.

Revere reached the Clark Parsonage in Lexington about midnight. He pounded hard on the door. He aroused John Hancock, who was no doubt wearing his moroccan slippers and India-styled silk jacket. Samuel Adams received Revere's alarm there, too. He and Hancock were the rebel leaders. Midway between Lexington and Concord, Paul was surrounder by redcoats with drawn pistols. There were threats. Revere became their prisoner. One of the Britishers, a sergeant, said his own horse was tired. He was given a fresher one — Revere's!

And that was the last the patriot saw of the horse which had given him the ride which was to become immortal.

Paul Revere's ride aroused America on that chill, moonlit spring night — aroused a stouthearted people to begin their fight for freedom. That ride was to become a symbol through centuries for a liberty-loving nation to keep on the alert. But tonight as I finish Esther Forbes' account of the ride, it carries, too, a new message:

Even when the hour seems urgent and the mission demanding, do not ride off in a frenzy. Do not panic. Ride with care. Ride prepared. Ride with a reserve for the unexpected ahead. Ride with a steady hand. That is how Paul Revere rode through the night on that most famous of all American rides.

ULTIMATUMS

THE YEAR 1959 PROBABLY WILL BE REMEMBERED in world history for its visits for peace between leaders of Soviet Russia and the United States.

The exchanges began during the chill of January with the tour of America by Russia's First Deputy Premier Anastas I. Mikoyan, an Armenian carpenter's son. Next followed visits by First Deputy Premier Frol Kozlov and the Soviet leader himself, Nikita Khrushchev.

To Russia jetted America's Vice President Richard M. Nixon.

There were memorable moments all during those visits. Perhaps one which will be remembered longest occurred on a July day near the gleaming, gold-domed central building at the United States' exhibit in Moscow's Sokoloniki Park. Mr. Khrushchev and Mr. Nixon were touring America's exhibit. They paused at a six-room model ranch house. As they viewed the many gadgets in the kitchen, the two broke into a spirited debate. It was the outgoing, roundish, plain-speaking former Russian miner against a much younger man — a black-haired lawyer son of a California grocer.

————————

November, 1959.

As the exchange warmed up, Mr. Nixon spoke boldly of the danger or ultimatums. He explained further: "What I mean is that the moment we place either one of these powerful nations, through an ultimatum, in a position where it has no choice but to accept dictation or fight, then you are playing with the most destructive force in the world." [1]

Vice President Nixon spoke to the leader of the Communistic world. But his warning about ultimatums is sound counsel for everyone.

Most of us are given at times to declaring hasty ultimatums. We have heard some of them:

"If you do that, I'll never speak to you again."

'If you will not permit me to go, I am going to leave home."

'I will resign if *that* happens."

"Once more, and you'll receive the worst spanking of your life."

To be resolute, to be determined, all will agree, is a great virtue. But it is foolish to make a hasty ultimatum which can have but one of two results: carrying out an unwise threat or by losing face by not carrying out the threat at all.

Luke does not say so, but it is entirely possible that the story of the Prodigal Son began with an ultimatum. So many similar stories nowadays begin that way. Too many ultimatums end as did the Prodigal story — or more tragically.

The account tells of the disappointment of the older, faithful brother in the "fatted calf" welcome given the

---

[1] See *Time*, Aug. 3, 1959, page 13.

wayward son.[2] But there are those [3] who believe the Prodigal suffered perhaps even more with the feast. He had come back ashamed, desiring only to be an unnoticed servant. But his grateful father had showered him with a fine robe, a ring, shoes for his feet and music and dancing and feasting.

No doubt the Prodigal's remaining days were happier than if he had stayed away. But his long, hard trek back is so typical of so many who begin their journey with a hasty ultimatum.

Only the other night a good friend of mine, responding to an invitation for a brief evening appointment, issued a hasty ultimatum. "Under no circumstances will I go," he said. Ways were pointed out in which he could arrange to go and still meet his other commitments. But he had issued his ultimatum. He had but two choices: carrying it out or losing face. He carried it out. But since then he repeatedly referred to the experience, seemingly with regret.

Some of the most gnawing, sleep-stealing hours of my life have resulted from my own hasty ultimatums.

Yes, on that warm July day in Moscow's park when Vice President Nixon courageously warned Nikita Khrushchev about ultimatums, he was speaking to me, also. Perhaps he was speaking to you, too.

----

[2] See *Luke* 15:11-32.
[3] Including Angela Thirkell. See Flesch, Rudolf, *The Book of Unusual Quotations*, New York, N. Y., Harper and Brothers Publishers, 1957 edition, page 227.

TRY !

A FRIEND [1] RETURNED THE OTHER DAY from a year-and-a-half stint in Hawaii. There he had been an executive in Henry J. Kaiser's renowned Hawaiian Village Hotel.

"One of my fondest memories of the islands is my association with Mr. Kaiser," my friend beamed. "I was in his home many times, and he invited us in for dinner on Christmas."

My friend continued: "Henry Kaiser is an unusual man in many ways. He is actually rather quiet and retiring. He is almost eighty now, but he still has the drive of a bulldozer. His working day begins at 5:30 a.m. It ends about 6 p.m. And things really move as he calls the plays."

"Mr. Kaiser once told me that 75 per cent of the things he tries fail," my friend continued. "He said he made up for these losses with the other 25 percent which succeed. For instance, his Kaiser-Frazer cars lost out in this country. But his automobiles are having great success in South America. 'The important thing,' Henry Kaiser told me, 'is to always keep trying.' "

———————

June, 1961.
[1] Enrico (Hank) Aloia.

There are many temptations today. One of the worst is the temptation to quit trying.

People have their opinions of Henry J. Kaiser. But all must agree that he has contributed much in his lifetime to the pursuit of freedom. A boy who left school in the eighth grade to help support his family, he startled the world by building 1,500 merchant ships during World War II. His mills during the war produced over a million tons of steel ingot and more than 20 million pounds of magnesium.[2] He became the world's largest manufacturer of cement, the third largest maker of aluminum. He has built homes at a pace of 80 a week. He helped build the Hoover and Grand Coulee dams and the world's largest water span, the San Francisco-Oakland Bay Bridge.

And as he approaches eighty, Henry J. Kaiser is still trying — hard.

"'It has always been one of my ambitions to 'build a business that knows no completion,' " he once said in a church sermon.[3]

He also recalled his mother's advice to him "from the days of my earliest memories:"

"'Henry, nothing is ever accomplished without work. If I left you nothing else but a will to work, I would leave you the most priceless gift.'"

But I keep going back to Mr. Kaiser's statement that 75 percent of his undertakings are failures. He is not afraid of failure. The important thing to him seems to be: keep trying.

_____

Forbes, B. C., *America's Fifty Foremost Business Leaders,* New York, N. Y., B. C. Forbes & Sons Publishing Company, Inc., 1948.

[3] Delivered at Marble Collegiat Church, New York; see *Reader's Digest,* January, 1950, pages 15-19.

When he was helping build the Grand Coulee Dam, largest in the world, slides threatened to delay the work. Henry Kaiser tried something new. He froze a hillside solid to keep it in place. When he was building the Shasta Dam in northern California, railroads refused to run a spur to his construction camp. He kept trying. This time he pushed a ten-mile conveyor belt right over the mountain.[4]

Yes, I should like to return to Hawaii soon. It would be wonderful to be lulled in the sun by the soothing rhythm of the rolling surf on Waikiki. It would be refreshing to sniff again the gentle sea breezes and feast on long, yellow strips of lush pineapple just in from the field. It would be great to catch once more the warmth of a red hibiscus perched over a smiling Polynesian face.

But this time in Hawaii, I should like to look for something else. At 5:30 a.m. I should like to catch a glimpse of a 79-year-old man starting his day — another day of earnest trying. I should like to watch Henry Kaiser start off, unafraid of failure and feasting on sweat with the morning dew.

That would be something — to witness in him that it is more glorious to keep trying than to find security. That would be *something* — yes, even sweeter than the moonlight melody of tender Hawaiian strings.

---

[4] *Time,* March 3, 1941, page 67.

STAN THE MAN . . .

Vernon Law, pitching star of the 1960 World Champion Pittsburgh Pirates, had been tossing baseball stories to us much of the day. We reveled in them.

"Tell us," my brother asked, "How do you pitch to Mays, Mantle, and Musial?"

I have already forgotten most of what Vern said during the day. But I hope I never lose his answer to that question.

Vern's V-shaped chin moved forward. His tall frame straightened. He spoke intently, without hesitation. "Mays has no noticeable weakness," he said. "He is a good breaking ball hitter. As for Mantle, he is always a dangerous, eager hitter, sometimes even swinging at bad balls. I throw him 'tight' stuff, right into the handle."

The Mormon pitcher spoke even more respectfully of Musial, as if before a Lincoln shrine. "I never give Musial my best pitch," he began. "He knows his pitchers well. He studies and catalogs them. He seems to wait for the best pitch of each. Take Elroy Face, for instance. His forked ball is his, and one of baseball's

---

July, 1961.

best. Face throws it by putting the ball between his fingers. As the ball approaches the batter, it dips deceptively. Stan waits for that forked ball. He often explodes it."

Vern turned his comments to another Pirate pitching ace. "Bob Friend's best pitch is his fast ball. Musial will let Bob's other, easier offerings pass by. But when the fast ball comes — well, Stan likes to lose it."

Stan Musial in 1958 became the eighth man in major league baseball history to hit safely 3,000 times. After 20 years in the big time, his lifetime batting average was a remarkable .335. He set a record for appearing in more consecutive games than any other player in National League history. He is now in his 21st baseball season.

Musial got his start in baseball in a smoky little mine and mill town in Pennsylvania. Originally he was a pitcher. From those humble beginnings he rose to become baseball's "last aristocrat." And, according to Vern Law, Stan has reached the summit through looking for the "tough pitch."

From the banks of the ancient Nile, lush with melons and figs and pomegranates, Moses looked to an untamed wilderness. There he would bring the former Israelite slaves to new power and glory.

'If there is a place on earth that nobody else wants, that's the place I am hunting for," Brigham Young said on a summer day in 1847. Then, in a cruel desert by a salty inland sea, he and his homeless people began building toward greatness.

Yes, Moses and Brigham Young looked for the 'tough ones," too. So did a stammering Athenian boy some twenty-four centuries ago. Tradition says that he put pebbles in his mouth. When the waves were "violently agitated," he stood on the seashore and spoke out. He practiced speech while running "up the steepest and most uneven walks." He looked for the "hard ones" to toughen and refine his speech. He was Demosthenes, who became one of the great orators of all time.

A brilliant young German, skilled at the organ, in philosophy, in letters, and in medicine, looked toward the dark, disease-ridden heart of primitive Africa. There he bulit a hospital, hope, and an honored name. He is Albert Schweitzer.

This week a businessman returned to our town on a brief vacation. Several years ago he sold his business for a handsome price. He could have looked to a life of Mediterranean and Caribbean cruises, drawing-room prestige, and social splendor. But he looked for a "tough one." At an age when most men think of retirement, he has gone back to school — to earn a Ph.D. 'It's plenty tough," he confided to a friend.

But, he no doubt agrees with Stan Musial. A reporter once asked Musial: "Don't you think, now that you've got it made, you ought to play it safe and quit?"

Stan the Man replied: "Play it safe? Listen, if you want that, if you're afraid, you shouldn't even start playing the game." [1]

––––––––

[1] *Newsweek*, July 1, 1957, pages 69-72.

BOULDER IN THE STREAM

THEY CALL THEM BLACKFISH. But they are really not fish at all. They are mammals, nursing their young. Actually, they are small whales. They travel in groups.

Blackfish measure from 15 to 20 feet long. Their black, torpedo-shaped bodies are streaked with white across their stomachs.

Blackfish roam wide through the oceans.

There are no doubt many benefits to Blackfish through traveling in groups or herds or schools. But tonight I am looking at a tragic picture in color. It portrays a dozen lifeless blackfish strewn across a sandy beach. The herd had apparently headed into shallow shoal water. All those handsome animals of the sea which followed the herd had become stranded — and met a writhing death.

There are people like Blackfish. There are others, rarer though, like a man whose body today rests near a little wood and mossy meadow in Wales. There is no tombstone. There is no inscribed marker. Over his remains is a green boulder from the nearby foaming stream.

———————

July, 1962.

It is an unusual grave. He was an unusual man. He followed the crowd much of the time. But he dared to be different on occasions. When he felt the group was getting into shoal water, he went his own way.

His name is David Lloyd George, Welsh leader of Britain in World War I and the peace that followed.

Like other tots in his Welsh village, fatherless Davy Lloyd began school at 3½ years.

But David as a youth learned that the way of others was not always the right one. In one of his greatest addresses, years later, at Caernarvon, Wales, he recalled:

"Yesterday I visited the old village where I was brought up. I wandered through the woods familiar to my boyhood. There I saw a child gathering sticks for firewood, and I thought of the hours which I have spent in the same pleasant and profitable occupation, for I also have been something of a 'backwoodsman.' And there was one experience taught me then which is of use to me today. I learnt as a child that it was little use going into the woods after a period of calm and fine weather, for I generally returned empty-handed; but after a great storm I always came back with an armful." [1]

To many people storms have their terrors. To David Lloyd George they were opportunities to gather armfuls.

He entered Parliament while yet in his twenties. He was poor. But he was proud. He was offered a place on the board of directors of a large London drapery firm. The fee was 300 guineas. To accept such directorships was a common practice of men of affairs in Britain.

But Lloyd George refused the customary offer, with contempt. "A guinea pig?" he said. "No, it has not come to that yet." [2]

[1] Speech delivered December 9, 1909.
[2] Owen, Frank, *Tempestuous Journey, Lloyd George, His Life and Times,* London, England, McGraw-Hill Book Company, Inc., 1955, page 64.

A storm broke out over his head as Prime Minister in the midst of World War I. Lloyd George indicated he was going to appoint a particular man Minister of Munitions. Other government leaders strenuously warned against the choice. Lloyd George's man had an "unfortunate record." Two war disasters had already been laid at his door.

But the Prime Minister, with the eye of an eagle and the mane of a lion, made the unpopular appointment. Finger-shaking cries went up across Britain. Newspapers protested. Bitter letters poured in. David Lloyd George had stood like a green boulder against the rushing stream. The allies went on to win the war, with the able, dogged help of Britain's maligned Minister of Munitions: Winston Churchill.

At the Prime Minister's residence on London's Downing Street, David Lloyd George had a framed, embroidered text over his bed. From *Job*, it read:

"There is a path which no fowl knoweth, and which the vulture's eye hath not seen." [3]

It was the path Lloyd George sometimes took — a path no fowl knew, nor any Blackfish either. It was the path of an independent soul. It was an untrod, unswum path, often stormy, of one who dared to be different.

—————————

[3] *Job* 28:7.

MAN WITH A DOCTRINE

TODAY I PAUSED AT THE DESK ON WHICH James Monroe signed his message to Congress containing the words which the world knows today as the Monroe Doctrine.

The desk reposes now in Monroe's original law office. It is in a long, 1½-story, red brick building with a low roof and small, green-shuttered windows. The building stands on a maple-shaded street in Fredericksburg, Virginia. When Monroe signed the historic message, the desk was in the White House in Washintgon, D. C.

The desk had been brought by Monroe from France 26 years before he signed the Monroe Doctrine message on December 2, 1823.

'Most everyone knows that the Monroe Doctrine aims to protect the independence of nations in the Western Hemisphere. Fewer know about a message in 1822 from President Monroe to his mentor, neighbor, and idol, Thomas Jefferson:

"There was danger in standing still or moving forward. I thought it was the wisest to risk that which was incident to the latter course." [1]

This week I have retraced many of the footsteps of

March, 1963.

[1] *Time,* November 2, 1962, page 15.

James Monroe: in colonial Williamsburg, where he studied with John Marshall at William and Mary; at Fredericksburg, where he practiced law; at Ash Lawn, which was his home so long in a white frame farmhouse designed for him by Jefferson and only two miles from Jefferson's Monticello; and the White House in Washington.

Monroe's ability does not impress you. He was not handsome but rather rawboned. He was six feet tall with square shoulders. It is said he was clumsy and lacked polish. You find in him little evidence of the inventive genius of Jefferson, the generalship of Washington, or the ability to think like Madison or write like Franklin. I tried reading parts of Monroe's autobiography.[2] The sentences are long and dull. He once submitted a manuscript for a book to a Judge Hay. Hay's appraisal: "I think your time could have been better employed." [3]

But as you move with him over the rolling, wooded hills of Virgina, where the oak grow tall, you are impressed with this about James Monroe:

He seemed to have a personal Monroe Doctrine. He expressed it as President in those lines to Jefferson: If there is danger in standing still or moving forward, move forward.

In that old law office hung his Revolutionary War rifle. Carved crudely on its stock were his initials, W-M (for William and Mary), and '76. He volunteered at 17 to fight with the colonists. He no doubt saw danger

---

[2] *The Autobiography of James Monroe*, edited by Stuart Gerry Brown, Syracuse, New York, Syracuse University Press, 1959.

[3] Moran, Thomas Francis, *American Presidents*, New York, N. Y., Thomas Y. Crowell Co., 1928, page 63.

at home or with the troops. He chose to move forward as a soldier. He was with Washington's ragged little army which crossed the Delaware in midwinter, marched nine miles through sleet and snow on Christmas night, and surprised the enemy the next morning at Trenton. Monroe, with the vanguard, volunteered to serve next to the captain in leading the group. When the captain was wounded, Monroe moved into command of the vanguard. He received a musket ball in his shoulder. But he had helped General George Washington on that day in 1776 score a brilliant turning-point victory in the fight for freedom.

Monroe's personal doctrine of moving forward as against standing still made him a hero. Thereafter he kept moving upward, sometimes stumbling badly. But he chose to keep moving. He held more high offices in government than any other American in history: member of the Continental Congress; United States Senator; envoy to France, Britain, and Spain; governor of Virginia, four terms; Secretary of State and Secretary of War (at same time); and twice President of the United States.

Perhaps the best evidence, though, of his personal doctrine was on that December day in 1823. He had been re-elected President, unopposed, for the second time. America was in the midst of "the era of good feeling." It could have been a time for James Monroe to relax and look back on 40 years of almost continual public service in high office. It was a tempting time to stand still. But his personal doctrine dictated otherwise. In his small, cramped handwriting on that brass-trimmed mahogany desk, he signed his name. He signed it to the resolute message which has moved other leaders and a nation to act boldly at times for generations since. His message contained America's Monroe Doctrine.

BOOK SIX

Make Me To Hear Joy

*"Make me to hear joy
and gladness; that the
bones which thou hast
broken may rejoice."*
—Psalms 51:8

WHAT KIND OF EGG?

IT IS AN UNUSUAL ADVERTISEMENT! [1]
It fills a large magazine page, but it is illustrated by
one small picture — of an egg. The advertisement's only
headline is the picture's caption: "The average egg."

The text begins: "To many people, eggs are eggs.
When you've seen one, you've seen them all."

The message continues to explain that some people
think of human beings as they do eggs — as statistics.
People are not numbers, the advertisement stresses.
Neither are eggs. Each is different. To illustrate the
point, it is explained that "the average egg" in that
picture turned out to be a female alligator.

An alligator's egg does look like a large hen's egg.
Some men look alike. So do some women. But they are
different, often as different as an alligator's egg and a
hen's egg. All of us at times are prone to look on men
and women as statistics. Too often we measure them
and treat them according to the positions they hold. Or
by the club to which they belong, or the house in which
they live, or the clothes which they wear.

Perhaps we should measure a man by the way he
measures up to the demands or opportunities of his

May, 1964.
[1] In *Advertising Age*, April 22, 1963, sponsored by Young & Rubicum, Advertising.

position, as high or humble as it may appear.

At a recent community meeting, a man introduced himself as being "unemployed." Actually he is. A modest man, he is retired with more than adequate means. More important, he is respected for hundreds of miles around his suburban home. He has directed one of the largest merchandising institutions in our city. He has held high positions in government. Lawmakers, governors, church leaders, and businessmen often continue to seek his advice. But if you measure him by his present position, he is unemployed.

Diogenes wandered barefoot through the streets of ancient Athens, and tradition says he used a tub for a shelter. He was once captured by pirates. They offered him for sale as a slave. Pointing to a wealthy Corinthian, Diogenes said: "Sell me to that man. He needs a master." The Corinthian bought him, and as a slave Diogenes did become a master. In fact, he so measured up to his position as a slave that he is known today as one of history's great philosophers.

Perhaps we err most in measuring children. It is a wise teacher or parent or friend who never writes off a boy or girl as a failure. Each one is different. Each one is a child of God, which means there is divinity in his soul.

When I attended grade school, in a two-story, purple-brick building on the outskirts of town, a brown-eyed girl was a student there. She was a year older than most of the others in her class. No doubt some thought she might have been held back a year because of poor school work. Her speech was a bit slow. Some were probably tempted to treat her accordingly. Only this week, some forty years later, I learned why she was a year behind. Now a successful mother and respected church and community leader, she told me what had happened: her father had kept her out of school a year to look after her mother, who had been ill for months before giving birth to a son.

Only yesterday another woman told me about her niece who attended the same school years ago. She was dark-eyed, black-haired, and strikingly beautiful. A boy in her neighborhood had cast eyes at her. But she would have nothing to do with him. "He looked too much like a hick," she explained. Today he is a national figure, respected by millions as a model family man, an eminent success in several chosen fields — and handsome, too!

You know of similar instances.

When we were boys, we sometimes heard the expression: "What kind of egg is he?" Boys and men and girls and women are like eggs. There are really few bad ones. But they are all different. Each needs different treatment. None should be measured like a statistic. After all, what we think is an ordinary hen's egg may turn out to be an alligator.

LET US REASON TOGETHER

I WAS LICKING MY WOUNDS.
An associate on a project had been hurt by my words.
I related the incident to a friend of many years. My
friend replied: "You commanded when you should
have counseled. After all, your associate had as much
right as you to make those decisions. Your decisions
were not necessarily wrong. In fact, your associate
would have probably gone along with you on each of
them — had you asked instead of commanded."

Actually my wise friend was saying what Isaiah, that
ancient prophet-statesman, had written:

"Come now, and let us reason together. . ." [1]

Alfred P. Sloan, Jr. has won his place as a genius in
organization in the world of business. This shy, slender,
sweat-loving son of a Brooklyn merchant guided the
world's largest manufacturing corporation, General
Motors, longer than any other man.[2] In his autobiography, *My Years with General Motors,*[3] Mr. Sloan
describes the rise of this mighty industrial empire and

August, 1964.
[1] *Isaiah* 1:18.
[2] Mr. Sloan was president of General Motors Corporation 1923-37, chairman of the
board 1937-56.
[3] Sloan, Alfred P., Jr., *My Years With General Motors,* Garden City, New York,
Doubleday & Company, Inc., 1964.

the organizational patterns and practices which have made it tick. Repeatedly through the book one catches the power of Isaiah's counsel: ". . . let us reason together."

Mr. Sloan describes the beginnings of General Motors in 1908, the same year Henry Ford announced the Model T. General Motor's founder was William C. Durant, an automotive wizard with rare imagination, generous human qualities, and high integrity. But, Mr. Sloan points out, Mr. Durant "overloaded himself." Important decisions had to wait until he was free, and then they were often made impulsively. There was not enough "let us reason together."

General Motors ran into financial troubles in 1920, when most of the corporation's divisions were overspending. Each division was out for itself. There was not enough "let us reason together" between the heads of Cadillac, Chevrolet, Buick, and other divisions.

General Motors, after a shaky infancy, became great, Mr. Sloan notes, "because of its people and the way they work together."

Once asked about his recipe for handling men, Mr. Sloan replied: "I never give orders. . . . Perhaps an executive, through years of building up confidence, might get to the point where he could afford to say, 'You do this because I ask you to.' But an executive is wrong so many times himself that this would be a dangerous course to follow. He would miss so many opportunities for obtaining wise counsel."

Mr. Sloan continued: "If people can get each other's point of view, disagreement as to policies and courses of action are usually slight." [4]

[4] Forbes, B. C. and O. D. Foster, *Automotive Giants of America,* New York, N.Y., B. C. Forbes Publishing Company, 1926, pages 237-239.

"Let us reason together" is vital in business. It is even more important in the home and classroom. Many a heartache and heartbreak comes because there are commands instead of reasoning together — between husband and wife, mother and daughter, father and son, and teacher and pupil.

The other day I called a friend for a donation to a political candidate's campaign. This friend is known as a tough, successful businessman. His reply: "I think I'll contribute. I am in sympathy. But before I give you my answer, I must talk it over with my wife."

I have known that man for decades. Hard fighting as he is on Main Street, he seems to enjoy a happy home. He and his wife apparently "reason together."

Another friend, a teacher, told me about getting close to a son on a mountain hike. And there was a woman who spent some of her most delightful moments in the wee hours visiting with her daughter upon the daughter's return from dates.

One of the most stimulating teachers I ever had was a thin, gray-haired instructor in English who pursued learning with us students as his partners. He led us to reason together in probing the art of writing. Study *with* him, rather than *for* him, became exciting.

I have long admired Isaiah. He was a poet who was practical, a prophet who looked, with God, centuries into the future. But this week my respect for Isaiah has reached a new high as I have read and reread his gem:

"Come now, and let us reason together. . . ."

WITH NO CRUTCHES

THIS WAS THE MORNING AFTER OUR ARRIVAL by car at Mazatlan, semi-tropical city deep down along Mexico's west coast.

Now we planned some morning shopping in town. We climbed into our yellow, four-door sedan. I turned the key. Nothing happened. The battery was dead. I immediately went to the hotel clerk, knowing he spoke English. (My Spanish vocabulary consisted of about six words.) I asked him if the hotel deliveryman could push me with his truck. I also inquired if a Mexican boy could go along with me to explain my needs to a garage repairman.

"All our boys are busy right now," the clerk said.

And this was where a long chain of happy, sometimes exciting experiences in Mexico began. I suddenly realized that by asking for a Mexican boy to go along I was seeking a crutch — someone to lean on.

Now I was on my own, in a strange country. I waved to a Mexican couple backing out of the hotel parking area. They gave my car a push, the motor started, and I was soon wandering through Mazatlan looking for a repair garage and hoping the motor would not die.

——————

October, 1963.

one hundred seventy-nine

In the suburbs, a large garage was found. The repairs completed, I asked the price. "A thousand pesos (about $80)," the crew cut receptionist [1] twinkled. Then he spoke his price: "Ten pesos."

On our own, one after another, we met kindly Mexican people. Often no words were understood. But we felt the closeness and warmness of their hearts.

There was a 16-year-old Mexican boy we met on the outskirts of cobbled, palmy San Blas, some thirty miles off the coast highway and centuries ago a Spanish port city. The boy wore a buttonless, white jacket with faded red stripes. His black hair was as long on the sides as on top. He was short, rather muscular. His big, brown eyes were quick. He spoke excellent English and knew a little German, too.

In a dugout boat hewn from mountain mahogany, he took us on a three-hour tour through a tropical jungle. We saw Mexican men, two to a small dugout, fishing with long spears or prongs on poles about ten feet long. "They are after red snapper, catfish, snook, or mullet," the boy said. "They fish with a submerged decoy — a wooden fish about three feet long with back painted brown and belly, white, with marbles for eyes and pieces of rubber for fins. Those fishermen will spear as much as 50 pounds of fish a day."

The boy, Armando Santiago, pointed through the dense mangrove thickets bordering the stream to mounds, about two feet high, of what looked like dark-brown sawdust — on the tree boughs. "They are colonies of termites," he explained. "Parrots lay their eggs in those mounds. When the young arrive, their food is nearby — termites."

―――――
[1] Fernando Dimayuga Parra.

Armando took us into the tropical growth to a mountain pool, fed by a gushing spring. We swam in the cool, bracing water. Deep in the tropics, a Mexican woman sold us delicious bananas from her grove for only pennies a bunch. An elderly Mexican farmer trimmed with his machete pineapples fresh from his field, sliced them and served us their golden, mouth-melting goodness.

We mingled and traded with Mexicans in the market places. Fears of a foreign land melted with their warmth.

Perhaps a brief sojourn through Mexico is like life generally. It is richer, more strengthening, and happier when we throw away our crutches and our fears, and go it unafraid.

Jesus as Jehovah of the Old Testament repeatedly told His people: ". . . Fear not. . . ."[2] He spoke those words to Abraham. To Isaac at Beersheba He repeated: ". . . fear not, for I am with thee. . . ."[3] To Jacob, after he had learned his son Joseph was alive, the Lord said: ". . . fear not to go down into Egypt; . . ."[4]

Jesus, in sending forth His Twelve into new lands, counseled them: ". . . fear not. . . ."[5]

Our Mexican trip really took on a glow in that hotel parking lot when I was forced to throw away my crutches and "fear not."

---

[2] *Genesis* 15:1.
[3] *Genesis* 26:24.
[4] *Genesis* 46:3.
[5] *Matthew* 10:28.

STRANGLER FIG

OUR BOAT PUSHED SLOWLY THROUGH
the lazy, yellow-brown stream in Florida's everglades.
We were looking for alligators.

Our eager eyes searched down the little avenues of
water feeding into the stream. We looked into the
tangled masses of tropical roots rising like boas out of
the muddy river banks. Here and there were lush and
leafy patches of lavender water flowers spreading over
the stream.

But no alligator raised his ugly head.

Occasionally along the stream we did see something
unusual. Our guide explained that it was a fig tree.
But it was no ordinary fig tree. It is called the strangler
fig.

The tree is well named.

Life for the strangler fig begins in the crotch of another
tree. In the case of a palm, the seed may have its start
in the center of a leaf. The beginning is innocent
enough. The seed is dropped by a bird. The young
seedling is slow in growth. Often the young fig derives
its moisture mainly from the damp Florida air.

Soon small roots are visible on the fig seedling. They

September, 1961.

grow downward along the bark of the host tree, or they may dangle in the air. The growth is slow, but the roots keep reaching downward. One day they make contact with the tropical earth.

Once a connection with the earth is made, the fig tree's growth becomes rapid. The roots increase in thickness. New roots are sent down. As the fig roots contact each other, they merge. Soon they form a solid girdle around the host tree's trunk. Now the fig tree is putting on its finery. There are long, dark green, feather-shaped leaves. Small reddish purple figs appear. They are edible, too. There may be two or more crops of figs a year.

But the fig as we saw it in the everglades is by this time a killer. Its girdle of roots begins squeezing the trunk of the host. In the end, the benefactor will die in the embrace of the guest. That is why it is called the strangler fig.

With a seemingly innocent beginning from a bird, the strangler will grow as high as fifty feet, and at times will spread over eighty feet.

Florida's everglades seem to be full of strangler figs. Life has many of them, too.

Strangler figs among men usually begin with kindness. At least the host thinks it is kindness. But if it is kindness, it is without wisdom.

The other night a troubled mother phoned. Her daughter's husband had left her and her family of little children. "Of course, my daughter is not without blame in this situation," the mother said. "But she is desperate."

I asked if her daughter was affiliated with the Church. The reply was, "No."

"When did she quit going to Sunday School?" I inquired. "When she was about ten," was the answer.

Perhaps that "strangler fig" situation began through a mother's trying to be kind to a daughter who did not wish to go to Sunday School. Perhaps the mother had felt it kind to let her daughter withdraw from the Church if she so wished — without parental encouragement to continue to attend.

Crime and trouble often begin so innocently, through parents thinking they are being kind by forever giving children their own way.

They tell a story in our neighborhood about a mother going to a wise friend. "I am perplexed," she said. "I heard my young son pray for a bicycle. I have no means to buy him a bicycle. What can I do?"

"Be thankful you do not have the money for a bicycle," the wise friend said. "Teach your son to pray, not for a bicycle, but for strength and ability to earn the bicycle he desires."

That wise friend was only reiterating what Jesus had said: ". . . be ye therefore wise as serpents, and harmless as doves." [1]

Wisdom with kindness is a great gift. Kindness without wisdom can plant the seed of a strangler fig — a destroyer that can eventually ruin even the life of the benefactor.

_____

[1] *Matthew* 10:16.

MARGIN OF MASTERY

IN RECENT DAYS THERE HAS BEEN coming back to me again and again a story I heard a speaker tell years ago. He spoke on preparation. Roughly the story is this:

A woman was purchasing a blanket. The clerk showed her a beautiful wool number. "Yes, I like that blanket very much," the woman said. "It is just what I'd like to buy. But it is too large. You see, my bed measures about five feet wide by six feet long. And this blanket you say measures eight by eight feet."

"But you should have this size blanket," the clerk answered. "You see, it is the extra footage — the part of the blanket hanging over the edges — which really gives you warmth."

The speaker then explained that it is a teacher's extra margin of preparation which really gives warmth to a lesson.

An able teacher was the featured speaker at Gettysburg on a late autumn day in 1863. Carl Sandburg has described him as "perhaps foremost of all distinguished American clasical orators." [1] He was Edward Everett.

_____

August, 1961.
[1] Sandburg, Carl, *Abraham Lincoln, The War Years, Vol. II,* New York, N. Y., Harcourt, Brace and Company, 1939, page 453.

When he had been notified in September that he would be speaker of the day at the Gettysburg dedication on October 23, he had asked for more time for preparation. And the dedication had been postponed until November 19.

Then there was he who followed Everett with "a few appropriate remarks." Abraham Lincoln, for his message which was to become immortal, had prepared long and hard, too. On the second Sunday before the Gettysburg ceremony when he was thinking about what he would say, he told a friend that his remarks would be "short, short, short, short." He was still polishing the night before the dedication, when he took his text for checking to his Secretary of State, William H. Seward. It was midnight or later when Lincoln finished working over his five-minute talk.

The evidence is that the Apostle Paul did not begin teaching the Gospel immediately after his conversion. For some three years he ". . . went into Arabia, . . ." [2] probably for long, hard preparation. Returning, he visited the first of the apostles, Peter, ". . . and abode with him fifteen days." [3] Paul gave his preparation the margin which brings mastery.

Paul once suggested that Timothy charge the people to do good, "Laying up in store for themselves a good foundation against the time to come, . . ." [4]

Paul, in his line to Timothy, tells me that men should strive for that same margin of mastery in fields beyond teaching. Take family finances. Generally a man is

---

[2] *Galatians* 1:17.
[3] *Galatians* 1:18.
[4] *I Timothy* 6:19.

happier if he buys a Ford when he can afford a Mercury, or a Corvair when he could get a Chevrolet. The resulting margin makes a man's pillow softer at night.

There are rewards, too, for seeking that margin in service to others, in speaking (by piling thoughts much higher than words), in driving on the highway, and in many other ways. Among them is prayer. Many men pray at night. They pray over their meals, too. Some men pray with their families in the morning. All this is good. But I like to think that there is a margin beyond that. It is the unscheduled prayer. But it is not a distress call. Mark describes one such prayer:

"And in the morning, rising up a great while before day, he went out, and departed into a solitary place, and there prayed." [5]

We are not told what Jesus prayed about on that morning before the dawn. We do know that afterward He went teaching throughout Galilee.

With blankets, they say, it is the margin hanging over the edge which brings real warmth. There is a margin in many other ways, from preparation to prayer, which warms the soul, too. It is the margin of mastery.

---

[5] *Mark* 1:35.

THEY THINK TALL

THIS WAS THE 35TH FLOOR OF THIS GLEAMING
Dallas bank building. For several days we had admired its towering walls of aluminum and glass. They
shone in the Texas sun like a bright new dollar.

Up here, now, on the building's 35th floor, our shoes
sank into carpet of deep green and light gold as we
moved through the bank officers' elegant dining room.
We admired the bleached mahogany walls, and then
looked out across the tall Dallas skyline.

Our guide was a pert young Texas woman in a dark
blue suit. She had a blond pony-tail, high cheeks and
deep-set, gray-green eyes that danced as she drawled.
"See those horses on that building over there?" she said.
She pointed to a double-sided neon figure of a large
flying horse advertising petroleum products. "There are
two of those horses so the folks over in Fort Worth won't
call Dallas a 'one-horse town.'" She explained that on
a clear day from this 35th floor you could see Fort
Worth, a big cow-town thirty miles away, "out where
the west begins."

But most of the time she talked about the wonders of
this tall Texas building. "Actually it is a 40-story build-

————————

February, 1960.

ing," she exclaimed, "if you count the four floors underground."

Her eyes really widened as she directed our view around the maple-paneled bank lobby. "It is almost as large as a football playing field," she said. And there was not a pillar nor post in it!

Some piece of Texas, that Republic National Bank Building! And it, together with its hostess, is so typical. Buildings *are* tall in Texas. (The Texas capitol in Austin is seven feet taller than the nation's in Washington.) It is true, much of Texas oozes with oil, but its buildings are tall in a large measure because Texans think that way.

Even an Idaho Russet potato seems bigger beside a Texas steak. And the potato probably is larger, because in Texas the white of a baked potato is whipped with butter until the jacket is bursting.

Tall Texas men wear tall white Texas hats. They wear tall boots, too.

They think tall in Texas.

Back in 1836, when hickory-hard Andrew Jackson was in the White House, one of his toughest Indian fighters was in Texas, still a province of Mexico. He was David Crockett, a mighty wilderness man with ax and rifle. People said that Davy could whip his weight in wildcats and outhug a bear. He was from Tennessee, but Davy thought and talked like a Texan. In the war with the Creeks, he kept Jackson men's spirits high with his campfire comics and tall tales.

In 1836 Texans faced a ruthless oppressor in Santa Anna, Mexican dictator. With from 4,000 to 6,000 soldiers, Anna marched into Texas. The call went out for "liberty or death" defenders. Davy Crockett was among those choosing to hold out at an old roofless mission in San Antonio called the Alamo. There were fewer than 200 men with Crockett at the Alamo. Santa Anna, with his legions, signaled for unconditional surrender. The Alamo's answer was a cannon shot. Then long rifles cracked. Crockett and the other defenders fought like the heroes of Thermopylae. Not one survived. Santa Anna, who lost from 600 to 800 men, in vengeance ordered the Alamo heroes' bodies burned.

Davy Crockett and other Alamo defenders could have chosen to flee. They chose liberty above life. They fought to the death.

Those Texans thought tall!

Little over a month later, a small Texas army heard a charge from their commander, Sam Houston: "Victory is certain! Trust in God and fear not! And remember the Alamo! Remember the Alamo!"

Houston's army surprised and smashed Santa Anna at San Jacinto. Texas independence was won. Sam became the Republic's first president. He later helped lead Texas into the Union. For nearly 14 years he represented his state in the United States Senate, whittling shavings endlessly on the Senate floor. But later, he vacated the office of Governor of Texas when its people elected to secede. Sam chose not to be governor and compromise his principles.

Sam Houston, the greatest Texan of them all, thought tall!

PROBLEMS OR CHALLENGES?

In a New York bank lobby there has been a display of pictures which has kept busy people lingering. It was the 28th annual exhibit of the Press Photographers of New York.

First-prize winner in the feature picture-story competition was a photograph entitled, "Closed — After One Performance." [1] The scene is in the shadows of a stage door. Sitting on the metal stairs just below the door is a pretty blonde. Her long hair is falling almost over her big, sunken eyes, as though anguished fingers had been running through it. On her lap one hand holds some papers. The girl's cheek leans against the steps' iron rail. Her tearful eyes speak hopelessness. She looks as though the roof of the world has just fallen in on her.

Most of us, no doubt, have felt, on occasions, as that girl looks.

The other night at dinner I sat next to a big Irishman who had been through an experience like that. He was tall, broad shouldered, and red haired. His freckles extended down to his finger nails.

As we chatted, his voice bothered me. It sounded like

July, 1964.
[1] Photographed by Neal Boenzi, *New York Times*, reproduced by *Editor & Publisher*, Mar. 7, 1964, page 53.

a phonograph record playing with a wornout needle.

As we visited and as he gave his dinner speech, the rasping effect of his voice melted away. All of us were charmed and lifted by this man, William Gargan. Briefly, this is the story he told:

While playing the role of the cancer-stricken ex-president of the United States in *The Best Man*, at a San Francisco theater, William Gargan's words became labored. His voice was husky. A biopsy showed cancer of the larynx.

Surgery resulted. William Gargan's voice box was removed in the autumn of 1960.

"I have never felt so depressed in my life," said William Gargan. "I had relied on my voice for years in movies, and on the stage, radio, and television. Now my voice was gone. In that hospital bed, I kept asking: 'Why me, God?' "

During his career as an actor he had earned over a million dollars.

One day shortly after he left the hospital, William Gargan was visited by a young woman who offered to give him lessons in what is known as esophageal speech.

"As I learned to speak again, I quit asking, 'Why me, God?' " he said. "I began saying, 'Why *not* me, God?' I realized I was in a wonderful position now to warn people to get checkups against cancer and to give encouragement to cancer victims."

Since 1960, William Gargan has been touring America, speaking as a volunteer for the American Cancer Society. He turned a depressing problem into an exciting challenge.

Actually there are no problems in life. There are

challenges. Some people make problems of them.

A poet son of an English bank clerk had more than his share of jolts. His first poem was "almost unnoticed." The British public ridiculed another of his works, *Sordello,* appearing seven years later. It was "likened unto a house built by a young architect who forgot that a staircase was necessary." He married an invalid against the bitter objections of her father, and she achieved more acclaim as a poet than her husband during their lifetimes.

But Robert Browning seemed to view all these reverses in his life as challenges rather than problems.

In the song of an Italian child silk-worker,[2] Browning wrote:

> "God's in His heaven —
> All's right with the world!"

Again, Browning penned:

> "Ah, but a man's reach should
> exceed his grasp,
> Or what's a heaven for?"[3]

On the day Robert Browning died in Venice in 1889, his poem *Epilogue to Asolando* was published in London. In it were these lines:

> "One who never turned his back
> but marched breast forward,
> Never doubted clouds would
> break."

The next time that "closed-after-one-performance" feeling comes my way, I hope I can remember William Gargan's "Why *not* me, God?" and Robert Browning's:

> "God's in His heaven —
> All's right with the world!"

---

[2] In *Pipa Passes.*
[3] In *Andrea del Sarto.*

WHEN THE ALPS ARE BITTER COLD

ALL MORNING LONG OUR ELECTRIC TROLLEY train wound through smiling little valleys and along sparkling streams and lakes bordered by tall evergreens and bursts of bright autumn leaves.

We were in the Bavarian Alps.

Early afternoon, we rolled into Innsbruck, a charming Austrian city cuddling near the towering hills.

The conductor thought we said *Vienna* instead of *Venice*, so we missed our train. That meant a delay in Innsbruck of over seven hours. But our misfortune had its rewards. For a modest price we bought handsome hand-knitted Tyrolian sweaters with gay designs. We enjoyed a sausage supper, too. And we feasted more on the Alpine scenery.

That was nearly a quarter of a century ago.

But the other day I read a piece about a sport in those Bavarian and Tyrolian Alps which made me want to go back and linger even longer.

The sport is the pursuit of the huchen (pronounced HOO-ken), "Europe's mightiest game fish." A land-locked salmon, the huchen has a fierce looking triangular head with reddish eyes and gaping mouth. His

———————

August, 1960.

one hundred ninety-four

back is copper color; his belly, silver. The huchen can reach six feet in length, 110 pounds. Even at 40 pounds, the fish fights like a tiger.

Yet, all the joys of landing a huchen come in misery. That is because this tough, spunky fish strikes not when the river banks are green, as we saw them. The huchen strikes in winter's bitter cold, when preparing to spawn in the spring. Those who pursue the fish must push through drifts and shiver for hours besides an icy stream, sometime watching the line through driving sleet. The fisherman's lure is of colored leather strings. His hand grips a huge reel. Often the shivering hours extend through weeks.

But it is a crowning moment when, after an hour of battling, the fisherman falls full length on a twisting, flipping huchen and smothers his prize in a snowbank!

The huchen fisherman seeks joy in misery.

Perhaps there can be joy for all of us in misery or misfortune — if we but seek it.

Only this week we heard a friend tell how her family had found hidden happiness in misfortune. She is a mother of nine children, all under 14. "Our seventh was born with a deformity," she said. "At the time we wondered what we had done to have this happen to us. We were depressed. But, now as the years pass we have discovered that this has been a blessed experience for us. Our other children have early learned, on their own initiative, genuine thoughtfulness and helpfulness. Ours is a happy home."

The other night tragedy struck a neighbor's home. The father died unexpectedly. Five girls from the neighborhod, all about 16, gathered at the home next morning. A daughter was their pal. Together the visitors moved through the house with broom and mop and cleaning cloths. They washed the dishes and cleaned the linen. From their homes they brought broiled chicken, baked potatoes, cooked vegetables, a salad, hot rolls and cherry pie. In misfortune, both the girls and a shaken family seemingly found a glow of lasting joy.

On the lighter side, Tish Whitney [1] told of her misfortune. After 18 married years, she prepared a dinner that was her worst. The meat was burned; the vegetables, overcooked; the salad, wilted. Silently, her husband sat through the meal. As she started to do the dishes, he embraced her tenderly. "What's that for?" she asked.

He answered: "Well, dear, tonight you cooked like a bride, so I thought I'd treat you like one."

Joy through misery!

Bitter winter, they say, is normally not the time to visit the Bavarian Alps — unless you love skiing or skating. But I would not mind — if I could catch a huchen; or, better still, if I could learn the art of forever seeking joy when misery or misfortune comes my way.

_____

[1] *Reader's Digest*, April, 1960, page 76.

"GO-GIVERS"

THIS HAD BEEN ANOTHER CONVENTION in the world's convention center — Chicago, that robust, folksy big city with a salty air and windblown hair.

There had been the usual talks by Congressmen and specialists in economics, public relations, finance, and international affairs. There had been impressive receptions and glittering entertainment and exhibits and seminars.

But I think what I shall remember best about that convention was a line from the youngest speaker [1] with the shortest talk at the general sessions. He was a young advertising and personnel assistant from Baltimore. He spoke on how financial institutions can increase their business. "What we need," he said, "are not so many go-getters, but more go-givers."

Business needs more "go-givers" all right. So does the world generally.

Since hearing that line in Chicago, I have wondered about the difference between an ordinary giver and a "go-giver." Yesterday a widow of many years gave me an answer.

March, 1962.
[1] Robert A. Mellendick, at the 69th annual convention, United States Savings and Loan League.

"When my husband passed away," she began, "a friend who had lost her husband shortly before told me that people would swarm around with kindness at the time of the funeral. Then, she said, the remembrances would fall off. The really lonely days would follow."

The widow continued: "But after these many years, that has not been entirely true in my case. Take one of my neighbors. He always saw that the snow was cleared from my paths during the winters. Then he moved away. But just today he came back — to clean up my yard. You see, workmen had a few days ago finished putting new linoleum in my kitchen. Scraps of old floor covering were piled in the rear of my home. My former neighbor took the scraps away in his truck. He also cleaned out old flower pots and left my yard tidy. On other trips to see me, he will change burned out light bulbs which his eyes catch. He does so many little things to help. And his kindness keeps repeating year after year after year.

"There are others, too," she smiled. "Two couples particularly have been so thoughtful through the years. They have taken me for car rides into the country. At times they call for me to go out to dinner. When my sister passed away, one of the women took me for a ride to take off the pressure. A similar kindness came while my daughter was undergoing surgery. Post cards continue to come from those folks when they are away on trips. They often call to inquire, to drop a word of encouragement. They always seem to be near when I need a lift.

"Then there is another thoughtful man," she recalled. "He was my husband's friend. Once a year, for 15 years now, he has brought a cake to my home — and he is a very busy business executive."

What is the difference between an ordinary giver and a "go-giver?" That woman would probably say that the ordinary giver gives once; a "go-giver's" kindness goes on and on. It goes beyond the funeral. It keeps repeating. It knows no end.

The greatest Giver of all gave that way. Matthew concludes his account of the earthly life of Jesus with His words to the Eleven on a mountain. To them, He concluded: ". . . And, lo, I am with you alway, even unto the end of the world. Amen." [2]

---

[2] *Matthew* 28:20.

BOOK SEVEN

Enter With Thanksgiving

*"Enter into his gates
with thanksgiving,
and unto his courts
with praise; be thankful
unto him, and bless
his name."*
—Psalms 100:4

SUMMIT OF LIFE

A FEW DAYS AGO, IN A COMMITTEE MEETING, a woman made a statement which has lingered with me. Red-haired and in her middle years, she [1] said, "Today we give so much emphasis to the youthful way of life. This is all well and good. But we need, too, to give more importance to age. We should give older people their rightful recognition."

As I reflect across the past, some of my richest experiences have been with those people in their later years.

One night some years ago, I was toiling late over my desk at the office. It had been a crowded, hectic day. I was trying to catch up.

A friend entered the room. She was the cleaning woman. She emptied a wastebasket or two and pushed her cloth over some of the office furniture. Her arms were long and thin and sinewy. And they were wizened with age.

We began to chat briefly. I confided to her the stress of having too much work. She straightened her tall, angular frame. "Don't ever complain about having too much work," she began. "It is not nearly as bad as not having enough to do. Believe me, I know." Then she went about her work.

January, 1964.
[1] Hortense H. Child.

That was a golden moment for me. Many times her words have come back tellingly to me. I shall always be grateful.

Then there was a man I never met until his hair was white as snow. We became friends for the last six months of his life. He filled me with words of wisdom. I line he liked to repeat was, "Keep your friendships in repair."

I recall a woman I met when her head was crowned with white. She had been a kindergarten teacher, and she told of a little girl who prayed for good weather on her approaching birthday. When the day arrived, the rains came. "The Lord did not answer your prayers, did He?" a friend chided her. "Yes, He did," the girl replied, "but He said, 'No.'"

That wisp of a woman told that story over twenty years ago, yet its message remains fresh today.

There are many others I have met in their sunset years. I enjoyed an elderly neighbor who raised plump strawberries and exquisite gladioli. Sage words, mingled with gardening hints, tumbled from his lips as he leaned against the white picket fence.

One of my most stimulating friends today is well into his eighties. He was a pioneer newspaper artist. He keeps very busy with his writing and talks of it as a boy with a new pony.

Few things are more refreshing than to pause from our hurry and to drink in the wisdom of one with the snows on his head. There is the summit of life.

President Hugh B. Brown once told of an experience he had as a young member of a bishopric in Canada. A woman who had sinned came before the bishopric.

They heard her story. Then the bishop asked his counselors for their recommendations. One counselor moved that she be excommunicated. Youthful Hugh B. Brown seconded the motion. Then the bishop,[2] old enough to be his young counselor's father, said: "It is good that God is an old man. I am going to forgive her."

The woman in committee meeting was right. Age needs more recognition for what it deserves, but even more for what it can give.

---

[2] Dennison E. Harris.

TENDER HEART

A GROUP OF US NEIGHBORS WITH OUR SONS today climbed a mountain trail to a hidden lake. We strolled among towering firs and beside gurgling streamlets spilling over rocks and through lush grass and brilliant splashes of wildflowers.

We paused now and again to view the rocky, snow-sided peaks above and the timbered and meadowed basin below.

After more than one of these pauses, I noticed that our six-year-old son sidled up to one of our neighbors and took his hand. For some distance they would climb hand-in-hand. Not a word was said. The neighbor [1] was a tall, erect young man with blond, crew cut hair. He is a successful young businessman and a church leader, too.

Why was our son drawn to him? Last night, while I was making campfire preparations, my young neighbor came along. He invited our son to go with him on a hike. He took an interest in our boy — and others, too. The young executive had taken with him on our outing not only his own son but another lad whose father was ill. Then there was another boy in the crowd whose

June, 1963.
[1] William Nathaniel Jones.

father was shy and did not usually go on trips of this kind. But the young leader had somehow quietly talked the father into coming along with his son.

I concluded that our son reached for the young leader's hand because the man had a tender heart.

Charles P. Steinmetz was an eccentric hunchback who has been called an "electrical wizard." A poor immigrant in America from Germany, he soon won acclaim for developing his theory of electrical currents. One bitter winter day a plant engineer climbed three flights to consult the genius in his small laboratory. He found Steinmetz, still in his twenties, toiling over his papers. He wore an overcoat, fur cap, and boots. His hands were blue with cold, and periodically he rubbed them hard so his fingers could work the pencil. There was no fire in his potbellied stove.

The engineer discussed his problem with Steinmetz. As the man was about to leave, he rallied enough courage to ask: "Mr. Steinmetz, why in the world don't you build a fire in your stove?"

The little genius replied apologetically: "Well, a mouse had babies in there; and they are not yet old enough to move." [2]

I like to think that much of the genius of Steinmetz came from a tender heart — a genuine desire to help others.

It is said that a struggling son of a drunken father was the composer who put a life-like soul into music. But he, Ludwig van Beethoven, was considered strange by many who knew him. He wandered through the woods and fields, sometimes sleeping wherever he happened to be. He was once arrested for vagrancy, and

_____

[2] Miller, Floyd, "The Hunchbacked Genius of Liberty Hall," *Reader's Digest,* June 1962, page 225.

often he wore his clothes until they were almost soiled rags. Too deaf to hear conversation, he lived a lonely life while masterpiece after masterpiece flowed from his pen.

But Beethoven was considerate, quietly. When one of his friends, the Baroness Ertmann, lost a child, Beethoven called on her. Saying nothing, he strolled to the piano. For a long period, he played music of comfort as only his genius could.[3]

Beethoven had a tender heart. Perhaps that is a reason he became the Shakespeare of music, the master who gave melody a soul.

I shall never forget the late Ruth May Fox telling me about an experience with President Brigham Young. She told me the incident not long before her death at 104 years. She recalled when she was a girl working in a woolen factory, the President inspected the plant. He paused beside her and asked: "How would you like to wear boy's clothes in this factory?" At the time, she thought he was joking. Later she realized that he was concerned about her dress getting caught in the machinery.

Perhaps much of Brigham Young's greatness as a leader came from a tender heart.

There have been tributes to lion-hearted men, and to stout-hearted men. But as I watched my son reach for my neighbor's hand and hold it as they climbed toward that hidden mountain lake, I realized: Few things are more powerful in influencing and leading men than a tender heart.

---

[3] Marek, George R., "Beethoven, the Incredible," *Reader's Digest*, August, 1962, page 179.

WHISTLER'S MOTHER

WE MUST HAVE SEEN IT THAT DAY IN PARIS over 26 years ago when we wandered through the Louvre, world's largest art museum. But my diary does not say so. After all, the Louvre covers 49 acres and its treasures include some 5,000 paintings.

But some day I hope to return and stand before that painting which for nearly a century has brought tears streaming down the cheeks of men.

The masterpiece is now known as *Whistler's Mother,* though that is not the name the artist gave it.

Today I have been searching into the biography [1] of the woman who was the subject of that painting: Anna McNeill Whistler.

She was daughter of a North Carolina physician of Scottish ancestry. She was 27 when she married George Washington Whistler. And when she went to the altar with him she became a mother of three. Anna McNeill had married George Whistler four years after his first wife died, leaving three children.

The children were soon calling Anna "Mother" instead of "Aunt Annie."

May, 1963.
[1]Mumford, Elizabeth, *Whistler's Mother,* Boston, Little, Brown & Co., 1939.

Anna's husband was a rising engineer in railroad building, who liked to play his flute to the family in the evening.

As George Whistler's reputation as a railroad builder grew, his family moved with each new opportunity. Their home shifted from New Jersey to Lowell, Massachusetts (where artist son James was born), to Stonington, Connecticut, to Springfield, Massachusetts. There, they were happy in a home overlooking the Connecticut River. They now had five children, three of them Anna's. (A son of George Whistler's first wife had died at 15 of typhoid fever.)

At Springfield a distinguished caller came to the Whistler home. He was a representative of the Russian government. He invited George Whistler to go to Russia as consulting engineer for a railroad to be built between Moscow and St. Petersburg (now Leningrad). It would be a long mission.

George Whistler turned to his wife: "The choice is yours, Annie," he said. She knew how he felt. It was a big, new challenge in the land of the Czar. There was no hesitation.

Anna Whistler waved a bright scarf as her husband sailed for Russia on a summer day in 1842. It would be a year before she and the family could join him.

Shortly after her husband left, scarlet fever took her 4-year-old son. On the way to Russia, she visited her sister living in England. She gave Anna a book for keeping her Russian diary. Into it, Anna wrote this quotation: "Gentleness is a mild atmosphere; it enters into a child's soul like sunshine into the rose bud — slowly but surely expanding into beauty and vigor."

As Anna and her four remaining children neared St. Petersburg, death snatched her youngest son.

The Whistlers were provided a home in a fashionable section of St. Petersburg.

After six years in Russia, the big blow came to Anna Whistler. Cholera took her husband. He was only 48. She accepted his death as a challenge, "to train our two lads to virtue such as their father's."

Twenty-two years later one of those sons, "Jemie," asked his mother to stand for a painting. She was now 67. She was too feeble to stand. So he requested that she sit "at her ease." He painted.

His work finished, he proudly called it *Arrangement in Grey and Black.* The painting became one of the world's masterpieces.

Ida M. Tarbell, the biographer of eminent men including Napoleon and Lincoln, was asked on her eightieth birthday to name the greatest characters she had ever met. Her reply: "Those nobody knows anything about."

Perhaps she was thinking of women like Anna McNeill Whistler, who devotedly helped her husband push to new heights and made selfless, able motherhood her career. Each of us knows a women like her. Fortunately, Whistler's mother had a son who could portray on canvas her soul. And that portrayal has become a symbol for other heroines like her — great characters who comparatively few people know anything about.

TO BE APPRECIATED

IT IS THIRTY YEARS NOW SINCE I QUIVERED under the thundering blows of a wooden paddle and entered a college fraternity.

Since then, there has been coming to our home, on occasion, a copy of the fraternity magazine. In the rush of events, each issue has been tossed aside, with hardly a glance. But a few days ago, a copy arrived with an article that stopped me. It was a report on a seminar conducted by the fraternity. Twelve young men from across the land, all campus leaders, were brought together to discuss: "The College Man — His Attitudes." They talked about education, careers, marriage, religion, military service, and other subjects. Their comments were taped. Excerpts were printed in the magazine.

One of the collegians said, "I want to be appreciated. That's more important to me than making a barrel full of money."

Everyone *does* want to be appreciated, whether young or old, high or low.

Time magazine, in reviewing Richard M. Nixon's *Six Crises,* noted how the former vice president "treasures tiny tributes as though they were sapphires." [1]

_____

August, 1962.

[1] *Time,* Mar. 30, 1962, page 14.

His book is sprinkled with little appreciations like these:

When the 1958 riots swirled around him in Lima, Peru, the New York *Times* Latin correspondent ran alongside the car, cheering: "Good going, Mr. Vice President, good going."

In Moscow in 1959, after the historic "kitchen debate" with Nikita Khrushchev, Ernie Barcella, correspondent for United Press International, whispered in Nixon's ear: "Good going, Mr. Vice President."

Following an address in New York City, as Nixon sat down, Governor Thomas E. Dewey grasped his hand, saying: "That was a terrific speech."

You get the feeling that these small acknowledgments were nudges which kept a world figure at his best, moving forward in tempestuous times.

There is a leader in our community who has built an honored name and a thriving business. What people perhaps admire most about him is his close-knit business organization, the loyalty of his employees in a tough, scurrying field where desertions are common.

One of his big secrets, his staff will tell you: little, unusual appreciations to both his customers and employees. Every employee receives at Christmas and on his birthday a personal gift from his boss, often with a "nice going" note. When the businessman goes on a trip, nearly every mail delivery brings an envelope for at least one employee — helps for his work, clippings from a faraway newspaper, or something else of special interest. The businessman is quick to pass along a note, often with a little memento, when a job has been well done.

These little gestures tell people they are important,

that they are appreciated.

People tell a story about W. Somerset Maugham, English playwright and novelist now nearing ninety, and the hotel where he always stayed in New York, the old Ritz-Carlton on Madison Avenue. On each visit he took the same sitting room and bedroom.

A friend, Jacques Chambrun, noticed an old cracked cup always rested atop a chest of drawers. He asked Maugham about the cup. The author then told this story. When France fell in 1940, several hundred English citizens living in south France were evacuated in two small cargo ships. The ships were crowded. The simmering summer sun made a furnace of the decks, as the ships zigzagged to avoid enemy submarines.

Each day's big moment came when the meager food was rationed out to weary, red-eyed passengers.

"That," Maugham said, pointing to the cup, "held my daily ration of water." He went on to say that now when he felt himself getting stuffy and unappreciative of life's goodness, he filled the cup at the water tap — and drank, slowly. "Brings me to earth in quite a hurry," he said.[2]

There is much in every man's life to appreciate. And there is nothing on this earth that deserves and desires appreciation more than a human soul. All around each of us are souls that feel with the college youth looking forward to a career:

"I want to be appreciated. That's more important to me than making a barrel full of money."

---

[2] *This Week Magazine*, August 22, 1954.

MASTER IN GIVING

ONE OF THESE THANKSGIVINGS
I should like to eat smoked Virginia ham with my meal,
then pause at an almost forgotten grave in an old
churchyard at Yorktown.

The setting is picturesque. To the west is the dark
green of Virginia's rolling wooded hills. To the east is
the blue of storied Chesapeake Bay. The setting is
historic, too. Here at Yorktown, Cornwallis surrendered
to Washington, ending the Revolutionary War. Only
about ten miles away is Jamestown, first permanent
English settlement in America.

Virginia's rich soil has given America many noble
sons, including eight American presidents.

But this grave is of none of these.

The grave belongs to a man named Nelson — Thomas
Nelson, Jr. He was a wealthy merchant, son of another
wealthy Virginian. He was a man big of body. But, as
John Adams described him, he was "alert and lively for
his weight."

Thomas Nelson was one of the signers of the Declaration of Independence. With his signature, he took the
pledge of its concluding lines: "And for the support of

————————

November, 1960.

two hundred fifteen

this Declaration . . . we mutually pledge to each other our Lives, our Fortunes, and our sacred Honor."

Thomas Nelson no doubt loved the mother country. As a boy he had studied at a private school in London, and he had been three years at Cambridge. But there was something he loved more: liberty. In 1776 he introduced in the Virginia convention the resolution calling upon Congress to declare the colonies free and independent. His fellow Virginian, Patrick Henry, joined him in advocating it.

The world would probably have heard more from Thomas Nelson had not ill health dogged him so. It caused him to leave Congress in 1777 and return to Virginia.

He was named commander of Virginia's armed forces. With great personal expenditure, he raised a large company and marched it to Philadelphia. The troops disbanded when Congress was unable to support them.

Nelson returned to Congress in 1779. But once again ill health took him back to Virginia. There, two years later, he was elected to succeed Thomas Jefferson as governor. Meanwhile, the war had gone poorly for the colonies. Their paper currency had become worthless. They were almost bankrupt. One of Washington's ablest generals, Benedict Arnold, had gone over to the enemy. Nelson had put up his own money to secure a Virginia loan in 1780 and for buying provisions for American troops.

Charles Cornwallis, the British commander, moved his army into Thomas Nelson's Yorktown. There, the British general set up staff headquarters in a three-story brick mansion with a high gable roof and two massive chimneys with heavily molded tops. It was the home of Thomas Nelson.

As Washington moved his troops against Cornwallis at Yorktown, Governor Nelson joined Washington with 3,000 Virginia militiamen. As the siege of Yorktown continued, Nelson directed cannon fire on Cornwallis' headquarters — Nelson's own home. One ball lodged between the gable windows. It remains there today.

Yorktown became a British Waterloo. Shortly thereafter, the redcoats surrendered, and America became really free.

What happened to Thomas Nelson? Ill health caused him to resign the governorship. The war left him poor, with a wife and 11 children. His fortune he had used for outfitting troops and for generally helping the American cause. He moved his family into a humble home in Virginia's interior.

Eight years after the war, an old enemy — asthma — brought death to Thomas Nelson.

My humble thanks go to that almost-forgotten man — for what he gave to bring freedom to me. My gratitude, too, for his lesson on *how* to give. Rather than leave his children social station and financial security, he chose to give them liberty and a good name. For that legacy, they, and freedom-loving people everywhere, have been richly blessed.

THANKSGIVING

IT WAS A BITTERLY COLD SUNDAY AFTERNOON. Climbing through the deep snow toward our mountain home, our blue and white station wagon stalled. It would not start. We were a long half mile from home. Our family began to hike.

A young neighbor stopped. "May I give you a lift home?" he inquired from his car.

"No, thanks. We're all right," I replied. Then waved him on.

We pushed through the snow. Arriving home, we found that the children's feet and hands were cold and wet. Some were numb.

"You should have accepted his offer," my wife said later. "Not so much that we were inconvenienced. But our friend probably went his way feeling we did not like him because we refused his kindness."

It is true that it is more blessed to give than to receive. But it is also often better to receive than not to receive.

There is an elderly woman we know. She has reared an outstanding family. They are all married now, and her husband has passed on. She lives a lonely and perhaps miserable life at times, because she does not wish

---

November, 1961.

others to "put themselves out" for her. Her self-pride and independence have gone to the extreme.

Perhaps she would enjoy Mona Gardner's story. Mrs. Gardner was at a summer retreat in northern Japan. It was on a cool, pine-fringed cove where families of missionaries and businessmen came to escape Tokyo's simmering heat.

Her 7-year-old daughter, Janet, came in from the surf complaining of a sore mouth. There was no doctor near. The girl's condition worsened. There was a half-mile walk, much of it over a cliff path, from the cottage to where a taxi would meet them. It would take them to the train for Tokyo. Fevered Janet was now too ill to make the walk.

Mrs. Gardner told some fishermen of her plight. They pulled their sampans ashore. Then they fastened ropes to Janet's iron cot. With Janet lying on the bed, the four fishermen carried it over the difficult cliff trail.

On the train, Mrs. Gardner asked to buy six full-fare tickets, so the seat cushions could be laid on the baggage car floor for a bed. The conductor disappeared. He returned soon, took Janet in his arms and asked her mother to follow. He led them to a private car. "The minister is sorry to hear of your child's grievous illness," a frocked secretary said. "He asks that you accept his bedroom."

At the next station, ice bags were brought aboard, requested by telegraph. While the train moved slowly across a sweltering plain, a coolie chopped ice for the stricken girl. Fresh blocks of ice were put aboard at each stop. There was no dining car on the train, but somehow the minister arranged for warm food to be served the Gardners.

When the train arrived in Tokyo, an ambulance waited.

Mrs. Gardner groped for words as she expressed thanks to Keinosuke Ushio, Japan's home minister.

Mona Gardner said that his kindness bound her to a code she has tried to live since: to try to help others, particularly those in need, as she travels to the far places of the world.[1]

From the candle of others' kindness to her she went about lighting others lives.

We have an elderly friend like that. For years he has been without an automobile. He graciously accepts others' offers for rides and other courtesies. He is always so grateful, it is a pleasure to help him. But his gratitude soon emerges into giving. He is a talented artist, and his personalized sketches are continually flowing to a wide circle of friends.

His life also seems to say:

It is good to receive, particularly when gratitude becomes a thanksgiving. And thanksgiving to many happy people is a linking of *thanks* to more *giving.*

----

[1] For more details, see *The Reader's Digest,* July, 1961, pages 37-40.

MOTHER OF FIFTEEN

TODAY I VISITED ONE OF THE TRULY SUCCESSFUL persons I have met. Her name is Mary Wright.[1] She has reached the summit in a realm where a woman should excel: motherhood.

Mary Wright is a Mormon mother of 15. She has more than fifty grandchildren. Yet, as she sat before her glowing splitstone fireplace, I could see no streaks of gray in her dark brown hair. Her bright brown eyes seemed to smile continually behind rimmed glasses. Hers is a smooth, peach blossom complexion. She is a prominent youth leader too.

There is not a scrub among her 11 sons and 4 daughters. All are under forty, but among them is a building contractor, college instructor, electronic engineer, manager of a wholesale distributing business, and a district manager of a large dairy. One son is a stake president. Several have served in bishoprics. Her 11 married children have all had temple marriages. Two of her children are now on missions for the Church. Eight others have completed missions, from New Zealand to France.

May, 1962.
[1] Mrs. Cleo D. Wright, 4288 South Fifth East, Salt Lake City, Utah.

"All of the children except the youngest contribute $20 each month to support our two missionaries," she said. My husband and I each add our $10, too — so it is easy on all of us."

She continued: "We have always done things together. As the children get married, the brothers join in helping build the new home. The real fun comes when it is time to paint. Wives and children join in the evening painting parties. There are hamburgers and chili, too. We often sing together as we stroke the brushes."

"What about housework for a large family?" I asked.

"It is easier than you think," she smiled. "In fact, when all 15 were at home, our house cleaning took just about two hours."

"Ever venture a family vacation?" I inquired.

"Yes, we have all gone together many times," she recalled. "You see, my husband has been a sheepman most of his life. We bundled all the family into his truck and headed for the hills."

I kept probing. For three years an invalid aunt was cared for in this busy, two-story brick home. Another time a cousin who was ill stayed here for some six months.

"What about disciplining?" I asked.

"Through 40 years and 15 children my husband and I have tried about everything," she chuckled. "Some things have worked better than others. When one of the children hurt another, my husband asked the offender to kiss the offended. That usually worked well. There were blushes and joking — and the trouble was soon forgotten. When children have left their things on the floor, I have asked them to give me a nickel. This usually corrected the problem, for a while at least. We have spanked occasionally — to let them know who was boss. We have not believed in threatening. We have never countenanced 'back talk.' We have tried to make all our work fun.

"One of the most difficult ages is 17-18," she said. 'I've chided our boys at that age. 'Do big things now,' I'd say. 'You'll never know as much as you do right now.'

"Another prickly problem is when a dating son or daughter gets serious with the wrong kind of person," she said. "We've never told our child to break up. But, we've let our feelings be known, and we have used patience and prayer.

"We discuss our family problems with our children, and we have had our financial setbacks, particularly during the Depression. One of our young sons, not yet married, came to his father once and said: 'Dad, let me have all your bills.' There was about $400 worth of them. The boy paid them all off himself."

"There is nothing like being a mother," she said. "A mother is a queen in her home. Motherhood is wonderful if you keep on top of it, and don't let it get on top of you."

I looked across the room at a grand piano. I glanced at needlework underway on her huge dining room table. I looked at shelves of books and magazines which caught her warm glances at times. She was on top of her job all right. She was on top of life. No wonder she smiled like a queen.

THE ART OF PRAISE

"YOU ARE MY KIND OF MAN; you remind me of someone I have met before," the rather short, nimble man said thoughtfully. His eyes sparkled behind rimless glasses. "I'll think of his name in a minute. He is a real power in his community."

Dr. Norman Vincent Peale was speaking to a businessman in our town. They chatted with others in the hotel dining room.

The businessman's face began to light up.

"Yes, I know who it is now," Dr. Peale added. "He is Louis B. Seltzer, editor of the Cleveland *Press.*"

For a good part of two days I watched and listened to Norman Vincent Peale as he chatted intimately with people in various walks of life in our city. He taught many of us many lessons. But the lesson which will probably linger longest with me is one he apparently did not realize he was even teaching.

It is in the art of giving a compliment.

His emphasis always seemed to be on the person with whom he was talking, rather than on himself. And when he commended, he told why, specifically — often with rare imagination, and always with the warm sincerity of the Ohio farm boy he once was.

March, 1964.

He had words of praise for the hotel service. Aware that the building was more than fifty years old, he added, "They must have a continual modernization program."

I introduced a newsman to Dr. Peale, telling him of a book the journalist had recently written. "I'd like your book," Dr. Peale said. "Will you send me a copy?" The newsman beamed.

Dr. Peale began his chat with President David O. McKay: "President McKay, how do you keep so young?" There were no lavish generalities. But, one by one, vigorously positive Dr. Peale bespoke his esteem with these and other comments:

"I have used the story of our visit six years ago in my writings and sermons."

"Your reference to the scripture on 'the little foxes, that spoil the vines,' [1] gives me an idea for a sermon."

Dr. Peale told of reading in the Book of Mormon about tithing, and how it moved him.

Before leaving President McKay, Dr. Peale asked him if he would offer a prayer.

But Norman Vincent Peale's art of praise perhaps reached its peak in references to Mrs. Peale — Ruth Stafford Peale — who accompanied him. Never did I hear him address her before others with such words as "darling" or "honey" or "sweetheart." But as we chatted, he tucked in lines which told his deep affection and great respect.

"Is it not true that you have written some of your books in a little retreat high in the Swiss Alps?" I asked.

—————————

[1] *Song of Solomon* 2:15.

"Yes," he replied.

"Do you take along two or three secretaries to assist you?" I continued.

"No, only Ruth," he said. "She does the job." Later he referred to her as "the real senior editor of *Guideposts*" (over one and a quarter million subscribers), the inspirational magazine in which they are listed as co-editors.

As the Peales were nearing the end of their visit, I apologized: "We have really run you ragged on your visit. Mrs. Peale is beginning to look tired."

There was no complaint. Then Dr. Peale added, hesitatingly, "She *is* getting weary, I'm afraid. Mrs. Peale's mother passed away last Sunday. The end was not unexpected, but it was debated whether we should cancel our engagement out here. Ruth wanted to keep our commitment. So the funeral was scheduled for Monday. Later that day we were on the plane, to meet my Tuesday morning speaking appointment."

What finer tribute could a master of praise give to her whom he loves most?

ADVENTURE NEXT DOOR

"Men Wanted for Hazardous Journey. Small wages, bitter cold, long months of complete darkness, constant danger, safe return doubtful. Honor and recognition in case of success."

That message is cited by the eminent copywriter, Hal Stebbins,[1] as one of the famous advertisements of the early Twentieth Century. Mr. Stebbins notes that the message was written by the Antarctic explorer, Sir Ernest H. Shackleton, and appeared in London newspapers.

The advertisement appeals to two desires in most men's hearts: for adventure and for recognition.

Irish born Ernest Shackleton found plenty of both in his 48 years. His expedition across the Antarctic continent in 1908-09 is said to be one of the most remarkable sledge exploits ever recorded. Reaching within 97 miles of the South Pole, his party was forced to turn back by violent storms and dwindling rations. He was knighted on his return to Britain. Honor came to him from societies in various parts of the world.

Sir Ernest completed another thrilling adventure in

November, 1964.

[1] "Advertising Copy — a Capsule History," Hal Stebbins, *Western Advertising*, published by Publishers West, Los Angeles, April, 1964, page 15.

Antarctica in 1914-15. His ship was crushed by ice in the Weddell Sea, and his party escaped in small boats to Elephant Island.

Not every man and woman has a particular yen to reach the South Pole. But most of us want our lives to be interesting — yes, even exciting. How do we make them so?

This week I have been reading the autobiography of the late Elsa Maxwell, "the reigning Queen of Party-givers." [2] George Bernard Shaw called this fun-loving and fun-giving woman "the eighth wonder of the world."

Of herself, Elsa Maxwell wrote: "I wake up every morning with the unshakable conviction that something wonderfully exciting is about to happen." [3] It usually did.

Miss Maxwell referred to her own life as a Twentieth Century Cinderella story — "and midnight has not struck yet." [4]

She was born in Keokuk, Iowa, across the Mississippi River from Nauvoo, Illinois. Her father was "an un-succesful insurance man," and she had less than two years of formal education. Her life apparently became exciting day in and day out, because she thought it would be and because of her intense desire to bring happiness to others in unusual ways.

Once in Cleveland she arranged for paper mustaches to be distributed at the door to sophisticated club women coming to hear her lecture. Her audience was captivated almost before she had said a word. At one party she

—————

[2] Maxwell, Elsa, *R.S.V.P., Elsa Maxwell's Own Story,* Boston, Massachusetts, Little Brown, and Company, 1954.
[3] *Ibid.,* page 15.
[4] *Ibid.,* page 29.

gave Albert Einstein — and other guests too — a thrill by asking the violinist in a string ensemble to let the scientist take his place in the quartet. The first party she gave for royalty cost $7, and was given in her two-room apartment, a converted London stable. Queen Victoria's daughter and 11 other guests were "put in stitches" with servings of boiled eggs and sausages and with the antics of four young troupers who included Noel Coward and Gertrude Lawrence. Teetotaling Miss Maxwell gave a group of distinguished bankers "the time of their lives" with a game played with a saucepan and corks on strings.

Many of us may not like parties as Elsa Maxwell did. But we can take a hint from her in the art of making our lives more exciting through using imagination in our kindnesses to others.

Some time ago when the mother in our home was ill, a neighbor woman quietly invited our 10-year-old son into her kitchen. For an afternoon she, with his help, baked bread. He came triumphantly home to his mother with warm loaves — gifts from him and our neighbor. Kindness with imagination!

This week we heard of a different approach to doing good by a group of youths. From door to door they went among neighbors asking for flowers from their gardens. The blooms gathered, they were assembled in attractive bouquets. Then the youths took them to patients in a local hospital.

Exciting days are at every man's doorstep. And there is no joy like that resulting from quiet, selfless kindness extended with a little imagination.

INDEX

-A-

Ability, 117
Abraham, 119, 181
Abraham Lincoln, The War Years,
  by Carl Sandburg, 185
Abraham, Plains of, 137
Accusers, 37
Ace, air, 54
Achievement, 116
Adams, John, 215
Adams, Samuel, 152
Administration, 27
Admiration, 146
Adulation, 104
Adventure, next door, 227ff
Advertisement, 173
  newspaper, 227
Advertising, television, 106
Advice, 61
Affairs, world, 58
Afghanistan, 102
Africa, 94, 162
Age, 203
  this wondrous, 90
  Agency, free, 62
Agriculture, Department of, 107
Agrippa, King, 106
Aid, foreign, 54
Aims, life's of Montcalm, 138
Airport, 54
Alamo, 190
Alexander the Great, by B. I. Wheeler, 103
Alexander the Great, 102, 103, 122
Alford, Clara, 97
Alfred the Great, 91
Alfred the Great, The Truth Teller,
  by B. A. Lees, 92
Alfred's, 133
Alligator, 173
Alligators, 182
Aloia, Enrico (Hank), 157
Alps, Bavarian, 194
  Italian, 124
  Swiss, 225
  when bitter cold, 194ff
Aluminum, 158
America, 100, 153, 168, 207
Americans, 52
American Cancer Society, 192
American Dairy Association, 51
American Kennell Club, 96
American Presidents, by T. F. Moran, 167
American Telephone and Telegraph
  Company, 105

Americanization of Edward Bok, The, 100
Amoz, 90
Angel, 25
Anger, 103, 146
Antartica, 228
Antelopes, 96
Apostles, Twelve, 24, 32
Appreciation, 212ff
Arab boy, story of, 47
Arabia, 186
Ardastra Gardens, 64
Aristotle, 122
Army, Montcalm's, 137
Army, Washington's, 168
Army, Wolfe's, 137
Arnold, Benedict, 216
Arrangement in Grey and Black, 211
Arrows, flying, 88
Artist, pioneer newspaper, 204
Artists, 117
Ash Lawn, 167
Ashton, Marged, 134
Ashton, Owen, 45, 141
Associate, 176
Asthma, 217
Athens, 106, 174
Attitude, "holier than thou," 91
Aunt, invalid, 222
Austin, Texas, 189
Austria, 66
Autobiography of James Monroe, The,
  by S. G. Brown, 167
Autobiography of William Allen White,
  The, 100
Autograph, 55
Automation, 68
Automotive Giants of America, by Forbes
  and Foster, 177
"Autumn," hymn, 43
Award, scholarship, 99

-B-

Babylon, 81
Bach, Johann Sebastian, 85
"Back talk," 223
"Backwoodsman," 164
Ball, forked, 160
Baltimore, Maryland, 197
Bank, New York, 191
Banker, 41, 85
Barcella, Ernie, 213
Barn, family, 113
Barnabas, 106
Barrister, Scottish, 114

Baseball, 87
Basketball, 36, 87
Bass, Sea, 30
Beach, sandy, 163
Bear Creek, 68
Bears, 113
Beatitudes, 37
Beckstead, Reed H., 58
Bed, hospital, 192
Bede, 91
Beersheba, 77, 181
Beethoven, Ludwig Von, 207, 208
Beggar, 121
Bel Air, California, 23
Belgium, 118
Ballamy, Francis Rufus, 146
Belshazzar, 81
Benefactor, 184
Best Man, The, 192
Bethany, 24
Bethesda, pool of, 24
Bethlehem, 20, 142
Betrayal, of Jesus, 33
Bevan, Aneurin, 52, 53
Bible, 96, 113, 119
Bird, 183
Birds, in the Bush, 76ff
Birth, 91
Birth, of Jesus, 24
Birthright, 103
Bishop, in Canada, 204
Biscuits, 92
Bitterness, 145
Black fish, 163, 165
Blair Street, 69
Blanket, 185
Blankets, 187
Blessings, 116
Blind man, at Bethsaida, 37
Blizzards, 88
Blonde, 191
Bloody Nose Ridge, 116
Bluebird, racing car, 123
Bluejay, 23
Boarders, 100
Boat, 182
Boat, dugout, 180
Bok, Edward William, 100
Boenzi, Neal, 191
Bombers, 117
Bombers, Nazi, 118
Bond, ship's, 43
Bonneville salt flats, 123
Book of Mormon, 225
Bortz, Dr. Edward L., 125
Boston, Massachusetts, 152

Boulder, green, 163
   in the stream, 163ff
Boy, 22
   Athenian, 161
   blind, adopted by couple, 92
   Dutch immigrant, 101
   dying, 107
   Mexican, 179
Boyhood, 120
Boy Scouts, 89
Brant, Irving, 73
Bread, 103
Breeds, of dogs, 96
Brevits, 111
Brickfields, Egypt's, 52
Bridge, San Francisco-Oakland Bay, 158
Britain, 91, 99, 149, 165, 168, 227
Britishers, 153
Brook, 143
Broom, 52
Brown, Hugh B., 119, 204, 205
Brown, Stuart Gerry, 167
Browning, Robert, 193
Buck, Frank, 81
Buick, 177
Building, engineering, 57
   office, 33
Bullbaiting, 97
Bulldog, 97
Bullet, sniper's, 116
Bus, double-deck, 144
Business, oil, 78
   world of, 176
Businessman, 22, 162
   thoughtful, 213
Byron, 115

-C-

Cabinet, Britain's, 52
Cadillac, 177
Caernarvon, Wales, 164
Cake, 199
"Calf, fatted," 155
California, northern, 19
Camp, Danish, 92
Campaign, political candidates', 178
Campbell, Donald, 123ff
Campbell, Sir Malcolm, 123ff
Canada, 204
Cancer, 27
   of larynx, 192
Capernaum, 37
Capitol, Texas, 189
Cardinals, birds, 40
Cards, post, 198
Car, speed, 123
   three-wheel electric, 129

Cars, cable, 133
Carousel, musical play, 36
Carpet, 188
  soaking wet, 130
Carthage, 104
Cats, 68
Causes, in the world, 20
Cedars of Lebanon, 133
Cement, 158
Centurion, 24
Centurion, Roman, 146
Chaldeans, 81
Challenges, 126
Chambrun, Jacques, 214
Champion, automobile racing, 54
Chance, second, 148ff
Chapel, little log, 67
Charlestown, 152
Charlestown Common, 152
Cheer, be of good, 33
Chesapeake Bay, 121, 215
Chesterton, G. K., 39
Chevrolet, 177, 187
Chicago, Illinois, 197
  University of, 125
Chik T' Sun of Caversham (dog), 97
Child, deformed, 195
Child, Hortense H., 203
Child, small, 37
Children, 195
  measuring, 174
Chinese, 97
Chinook, salmon, 30
Cholera, 211
Christian, 92
Christmas, 26, 213
Christmas Eve, 22
  first, 36
  spirit of, 129
Christopher Columbus, Mariner, by
  S. E. Morrison, 65
Church, 175, 184
Churchill, Winston, 53, 165
Clairborne, Governor, 149
Clark Parsonage, 152
Class, chemistry, 116
Clemens, Jane Lampton, 68
Clerk, hotel, 179
Cleveland, Ohio, 228
Cleveland *Press,* 224
Clitus, death of, 103
Clouds, 35
Coal, earth's supply, 112
Coat, 134
Colorado, 69
Colton, Don B., 41
Columbus, 63, 65

"Come, Come Ye Saints," music, 44
Comics, campfire, 189
Compliment, art of guiding a, 224
Comfort, messages of, 32
"Comin' Round the Mountain,"
  music, 44
Competition, 33
Concerts, summer, 42
Concord, 153
Conference, press, 54
Congo, 84
Congressman, former, 41
Congressmen, 197
Connecticut River, 210
Constitution, of the U. S., 73
Constitutional Convention, 74
Continent, American, 111
Continental Congress, 168
Convention, 197
Convention, Virginia, 216
Conveyor, ten-mile, 159
Conway, Walter, 53
Cora, 40
Corianthian, 174
Cornwallis, Charles, 215, 216, 217
Correspondent, Latin, 213
Corvair, 187
Country, Christmas Tree, 127ff
Couple, struggling to pay off debt, 92
Courage, 34
Court, Denver's juvenile, 71
Court, king's, 82
Court, Macedonia, 122
Cousins, country, 89
Cow, Counsel from a, 51ff
Coward, Noel, 229
Creeks, indians, 189
Crew, construction, 47
Crickets, 42
Crime, 184
  juvenile, 74
Crises, three in Daniel's life, 82
Crockett, Davis, 189
Cross, 24
Crowd, fast, 70
Cruise, Caribbean, 162
Cruise, Mediterranean, 162
Crutches, with no, 179ff
Cub, black, 95
Cuba, 54
Cuckoo, European, 39
Currency, 216
Currents, theory of electrical, 207
Cutler, Dr. Virginia F., 115
Czar, land of, 120

-D-

Dairyman, 51
Dallas, Texas, 188
Danes, 91
Daniel, 81ff
Daniel, Book of, 81
Darius, the Median, 81, 83
Daughter, 183
Daughters, of author, 63
David, story of, 141ff
Day, nerve-knocking, 125
Debate, between Nixon and Krushchev, 154
Debate, kitchen, 213
Debt, National, 54
de Champlain, Samuel, 136
de Montcalm, Marquis, 136
Declaration of Independence, 215
Defeat, 46
Delaware, 168
Delinquent, young, 71
Demosthenes, 162
Den, lion's, 81
Depression, 223
  spears of, 104
Desert, 94, 161
Despair, 103
Devil, praying for, 68
Dewey, Thomas E., 213
Diary, Russian, 210
Dichter, Dr. Ernest, 66
Diety, kinship with, 71
Digest, Reader's, 44, 53
Dignity, personal, 86
Diogenes, 174
Dirksen, Everett McKinley, 112, 113
Disappointment, 116
Disaster, real, 132
Discipline, 222
  in Sunday School class, 41
Disease, incurable, 114
  rare, 115
Disorder, 41
Doctor, 35, 45, 114
Doctors, 67
Doctrine, man with a, 166ff
Doctrine, Monroe, 166, 169
Document, British, 149
Dog, Top, 96ff
Dogs, 67, 96, 97, 98
Donation, 178
Donna, 26ff
Door, stage, 191
Doughty, A., 138
Doves, 184
Downing Street, 165
Dream, A Midsummer Night's, 85

Dream, of Nebuchadnezzar, 82
Durango, Colorado, 69
Durant, William C,, 177
Dublin, 20
Duck, 129
Dump, slag, 120
Dun's Review and Modern Industry, 105
du Pont, E. I. de Nemours & Co., 111
Dutton, William S., 44
Dye, M. L., 130

-E-

Easter, 32
Eastern Air Lines, 54
Eccles, George S., 93
Ecclesiastes, author of, 46
Ecstacy, 102
Edison, Thomas Alva, 59
Editor & Publisher, 107
Editor, country, 100
Editor, newspaper, 100
Editorial, 84
Edwards, Hedley, 65
Egg, what kind of an?, 173ff
  alligator's, 173
  hen's, 173
  oyster, 121
  of parrots, 180
Einstein, Albert, 229
Eisenhower, Dwight D., 34, 84
Elah, Valley of, 141
Eldorado, Kansas, 100
Electricity, 130
Elephant Island, 228
Elevator, 55
Eliab, 143
Empire Street, 69
Enemies, 34
Engine, diesel, 95
Engineer, 210
England, 123, 210
England, Ecclesiastical History of,
  by Bade, 91
Egypt, 77, 181
Egyptians, 96
Ephesians, 106
Epilogveto Asolando, by R. Browning, 193
Ertmann, Baroness, 208
Esau, 103
Esteem, 145
Eternity, scales of, 86
  with the family, 21
Europe, in 1936, 117
European Mission, 57
Everett, Edward, 185
Everglades, Florida, 182
Executive, 177

Executive, young, 102, 206
Exhibits, 197
Experience, exciting, 99
Experiences, in Mexico, 179

-F-

Face, Elroy, 160
Face, Polynesian, 159
Factory, woolen, 208
Failure, 158
Fairway, Golf, 57
Faith, 33, 56, 116, 143
 of a mustard seed, 24
Family, 21, 127
 close-knit, 70
 of Mary Wright, 221
Fare, adult, 88
Farm, Grandfather's, 115
Father, 19
 author's, 47
Father, Heavenly, 23
Father, unexpected death of a, 195
Fatherless, 91
Fence, picket, 204
Fertilizer, production, 22
Festival, 102
Fig, strangler, 182ff
Fighter, champion, 33
Fighting, 87
Figure, national, 175
Finances, family, 186
Findley, May Broomhead, 41
Fir, Douglas, 127
Fire, 130
Fireman, 130
Firewood, 164
Firm, London drapery, 164
Fisherman, big, 37
 huchen, 195
 Japanese, 219
Fishermen, Mexican, 180
Fisherman's Wharf, 133
Fish and Chips, 30
Fishes, 32
Fixture, broken lighting, 130
Flamingo, birds, 64
Flamingos, Nassau's marching, 65
Flathead Lake, 127
Flesch, Rudolph, 156
Flood, 20
Floor, ocean, 121
Flooring, Oak, 19
Florida, 63, 182
Flowers, 128
Folks, farm, 68
Folly, kingman's, 131
Food, rich, 82

Food, simple, 82
Foot, 130
Footsteps, of Jesus, 23
Forbes, B. C., 177
Forbes, Esther, 151
Ford, 187
Ford, Henry, 177
Forest, Kootenai, 127
Forgiveness, 132
Fort Worth, Texas, 188
Fortress, 102
Forty Famous Composers, by H. Thomas
 and D. L. Thomas, 86
Foster, O. D., 177
Foster, Sir August, 74
Foster, Will A., 51
Fox, Ruth May, 208
Foxhounds, 97
France, 117, 137, 166, 168, 214, 221
Francis, Saint of Assisi, 28
Frankincense, 26
Franklin, Benjamin, 74, 111, 167
Franklin, Mrs. Walter S., 44
Fraternity, college, 212
Freckles, Keep the, 66ff
Fredrick the Great, 85
Fredericksborg, Virginia, 166
Freedom, 94
Freedom, the fight for, 168
 price of, 95
 pursuit of, 158
 ride to, 151ff
French fries, 22
Friend, Bob, 161
Friend, of author's, 70
 business, 145
 busy, 67
 silver-haired, 123
 who drank, 70
Friendships, keep in repair, 204
Fringes, eat on the, 51, 52
Fruit, fresh, 107
Fullmer, Gene, 33
Funeral, 226
Funerals, tributes at, 41
Furrow, irrigation, 40
Future, 22

-G-

Galilee, 34, 187
Gallery, National Portrait, 144
Garden, 128
Gardens, Japanese, 133
Gardiner, Mrs. Dan S. (Phyllis), 95
Gardner, Janet, 219
Gardner, Mone, 219
Gargan, William, 192, 193

Gate, Golden, 135
  by the Golden, 133ff
Geese, young, 94
General Motors Corporation, 105, 176ff
Genesis, 132
Gentleness, 210
George, David Lloyd, 164, 165
German, 138
Germany, 117, 207
Gethsemane, 23
Gettysburg, 185
Gift, from boss, 213
Gift, No Finer, 35ff
Gifts, 36
Gifts, divine, 62
Gilliam, Judge Philip B., 71
Girl, little, 204
  student, 174
  teen-age, 155
Gladioli, 204
Glick, Ruth (Mrs. Harry L.), 41
Glow and Grow, 39ff
Goal, 99
God, 55, 82, 116, 178
  child of, 174
  relationship with, 71
Godhood, 24
"Go-Givers," 197ff
Gothe, 85
Gold, 26, 93, 94
Golden Gate Park, 133
Goliath, story of, 141ff
Goslings, 94
Gospel, 186
Government, Russian, 210
  of the United States, 73
Graciousness, grateful, 64
Grand Coulee Dam, 158
Grand Isle, 149
Grandmothers, hatpin, 89
Granicus River, 103
Gratitude, to God, 65
Grave, of David Lloyd George, 164
Grave, forgotten, 215
Gray Ladies, of music, 44
Greatness, Time for, 81ff
Greece, 121
  children from, 41
Greek, 138
Green River, 94
Greenwalt, Crawford H., 111
Greenwood, Donna Boyack
  (Mrs. B. R.), 26
Greyhounds, 96
Griddle, iron, 128
Grocery, corner, 134
Groceryman, 100

Guide, in bank, 188
Guideposts, 226
Gunboats, American, 150

-H-

Halibut, 31
Ham, Virginia, 215
Hamilton, Alexander, 74
Hammerstein, Oscar II, 35, 36
Hancock, John, 152
Hand, artificial, 128
Hannibal, 104
Happiness, 20, 116
  in misfortune, 195
Haran, well of, 131
Harp, 44
Harper, 92
Harpist, 142
Harris, Dennison E., 205
Hartley, Wallace Henry, 43
Haslam, Robert, 88
Hat, straw, 64
Hats, straw beach, 63
Hawaii, 157, 159
Hawaiian Village Hotel, 157
Hawthorne, 42
Hay, Judge, 167
Health, poor, 131
Heartache, 178
Heart, tender, 206ff
Hearts, Pharisees, 23
Heaven, kingdom of, 23
Heavenly Father, 21
Height, of redwoods, 20
Hen, 173
Henry, Patrick, 74, 216
Hero, where he lost, 136ff
Hike, mountain, 178
"Hill, Purgatory," 177
Hilton, Conrad Nicholson, 23
Historians, 96
Hitler, 117, 118
Hobson, Laura Z., 20
Hogs, 67
Hole, swimming, 89
Holiday, fishing boat, 29
Holland, 101, 118
Holt, Henry and Company, 42
Home, 218
  boyhood, 81
  frame, 19
  mission, 116
  peasant's, 92
Homes, 158
Homework, 72ff
Hoover Dam, 158
Hope, 36ff

Hope, messages of, 36
  to the world, 24
Hopes, Wings for Your, 111ff
Hopelessness, 191
Horses, dray, 20
Hour, David's finest, 141ff
House of Commons, 53
Houston, Sam, 190
Hotel chain, 23
Hubbard, Elbert, 86
Huchen, 194ff
Hudson River, 66
Human beings, 173
Hunchback, 207
Hunger, 103
Hurricane, Utah, 76
Husband, who died, 115

-I-

Iceberg, 43
Illinois, 112
Illness, severe, 114
Illustrator, young, 89
Imagination, 229
Immigrant, 207
Independence, Texas, 190
Indianapolis Speedway, Inc., 54
Indians, 88
Individualistic, 67
Industry, American, 105
Injury, 131
  crippling, 115
Innsbruck, Austria, 194
Institute for Motivational Research, 66
Institution, financial, 130, 197
Instructor, English, 178
International News Service, 20
Invalid, 193
Invasion, 117
Irishman, 191
Irving, Washington, 72
Isaac, 103, 119
Isaiah, 90ff, 176, 178, 181
Isaiah, Book of, 90
Isle, coral, 116
Israel, 52
  armies of, 141
Israelites, 97
Ivanhoe, by Sir Walter Scott, 115

-J-

Jacob, 77, 119, 131, 132, 181
Jackson, Andrew, 46, 150, 189
Jackson, The Life of Andrew, 46
Jailer, 106
James, Marquis, 46
Jamestown, 215

Japan, 219
Jefferson, Thomas, 73, 111, 166, 216, 81
Jerusalem, 81, 90
Jesse, sons of, 142
Jesus, 20, 23, 26, 32, 34, 37, 112, 146,
  181, 184, 199
  birth of, 26ff
Jevons, economist, 112
Jew, German, 84
Job, 19, 165
Job, toughest in the world, 34
Jones, William Nathaniel, 206
Jordan, 52
Joseph, 26, 77, 119, 132, 181
Joshua, 52
Journal, Wall Street, 22
Journey, hazardous, 227
Joy, 126
Judas Iscariot, 112
Judge, neighborhood, 60
Judgment, 84
Jungle, tropical, 180
Justice, Supreme Court, 99

-K-

Kaiser, Henry J., 157ff
Kaiser-Frazer, cars, 157
Kan's, 133
Keane, New Hampshire, 34
Kennedy, Joe, 101
Kennedy, John F., 101
Kenya, Mount, 93
Keokuk, Iowa, 228
Kindness, with imagination, 229
Kindnesses, 229
King and I, The, musical play, 36
Kinsman, kingly, 21
Kinsmen, love of, 34
Kings, They Made Others, 90ff
Kolby, Am, 128, 129
Kolby, Bess, 128, 129
Korea, 54
Koz lov, Frol, 154
Krushchev, Nikita, 154, 155, 156, 213

-L-

Laban, 132
Lad: A Dog, by A. P. Terhune, 96
Ladies Home Journal, The, 101
Lafitte, Jean, 148, 149, 150
Lake, hidden, 206
  salty, 120
Lameness, 114
Lamppost, 89
Language, common, 93
Lassie Come Home, by E. Knight, 96
Last Supper, 24, 112

Law, 73
Law, Vernon, 160ff
Lawrence, Gertrude, 229
Lazarus, 37
  death of, 23
Lead, pot of hot, 47
Leader, 119, 175
  Church and community, 70
  community, 213
  wise, 52
Leah, 132
Lee, Richard Henry, 74
Lees, Beatrice Adelaide, 92
Lentils, 103
Lepers, ten, 37
Lesson, as a boy, 47
Lessons, unforgettable, 57
Letters, Aunt's, 36
Levis, 87
Lexington, 152
Liberty, 190, 217
Life, summit of, 203ff
  tribal, 94
  youthful way of, 203
Lima, Peru, 213
Lincoln, Abraham, 33, 99, 112, 186, 211
Lions, Among Men, 105ff
*Little Journeys to the Homes of Great
  Musicians,* by Elbert Hubbard, 86
Loaves, 32
Lobby, hotel, 22
Locker, boat, 31
London, England, 57, 123, 216
  rebel in, 144ff
Lord, 55, 77, 181
Lord, Walter, 42
Louisiana, governor of, 148
  military leaders of, 149
Louvre, 209
Lowell, Massachusetts, 210
Luke, 155
Lumber yard, 19
Luncheon, civic, 56
Lure, fisherman's, 195
Lyceum, 122

-M-

Macedonia, 102
Madison Square Garden, 97
Madison, James, 72ff
Madison, James, by I. Brant, 73, 75
Madison, The Complete, by S. K. Padover,
  72
Magazine, 92, 120
  fraternity, 212
Maggiore, Lake, 124
Maginot Lines, 117ff

Magnesium, 158
Maharabal, 104
Mail, 88
  coat of, 141
Main Street, 178
Mallfactor, 24
Mammals, 163
Man, 204
  and his family, 21
  Chinese, 134
  deaf, 33
  overzealous, 52
  measuring, 173
  telling achievements of his father, 119
  thoughtful, 198
  who died, 117
  who operates downtown garage, 111
  with golden tongue, 119
  with withered hand, 37
  "unemployed," 174
Man, When a Boy Becomes a, 87ff
Manager, 26
Mansion, 23
Mansions, 24
Mantle, Mickey, 160
Manuscript, forgotten, 85
Marbles, 60
Marek, George R., 208
Marian, author's wife, 63
Marine, 116
Mark, 187
Mark Twain's Autobiography, 68
Mars Hill, 106
Marshall, George, 99
Marshall, John, 167
Marshmallow Sticks, 129
Martha, of Bethany, 37
Martinez, Al, 107
Mary, 26
Mason, George, 74
Master, in giving, 215
Mastery, margin of, 185ff
Matthew, 33, 199
Maturity, youthful, 84ff
Maughan, W. Somerset, 214
Maxwell, Elsa, 228, 229
Mayor, 60
Mays, Willie, 160
Mazatlan, Mexico, 179ff
McKay, David O., 225
Meeting, committee, 203
  community, 174
Mellendick, Robert A., 197
Men, colored, 93
  lion-hearted, 208
  wise, 82, 112
Mendelssohn, Felix, 85, 86

Merchant, Brooklyn, 176
Mercury, 187
Merrill, Joseph F., 57
Message, 119
Meteors, 39
Messiah, Handel's, 90
Mexico, 179
Mice, 20
Mikoyan, Anastas I., 154
Miller, Floyd, 207
Milton, 121
Mind, brilliant, 73
Mind, calm, 104
  mature, 84
Minds, three of world's great, 121
Mines, 93
Mink, 129
Minister of Munitions, 165
Minister, Japanese, 219
Ministry, earthly of Jesus, 32
Mischief, summer, 19
Minute Men, 152
Misery, 195
Misfortune, 131, 132, 195, 196
Miskelly, Sandra, 34
Missionaries, 222
Missionary, 123
Mississippi River, 150, 228
Money, 119
  why people save, 66
Monroe, James, 74, 166, 167, 168
Montana, northwest, 127
Montcalm Hotel, 136
Montcalm Square, 136
Monticello, 167
Morality, 121
Morals, good, 138
Morab, Thomas Francis, 167
Morison, Samuel Eliot, 65
Mormons, 116
Moscow, Russia, 210
Moses, 34, 91, 161
  death of, 52
Mother, 40, 184, 223
  of fifteen, 221ff
  ill, 229
  troubled, 183
Mother, Whistler's, 209ff
Motherhood, 211, 221
Mouse, 207
Moyle, Henry D., 78
Multitude, 32
Musial, Stan, 160, 161, 162
Music, 85
  a comforter, 42
Mustaches, paper, 228
Myrrh, 26

My Years With General Motors, by
  A. P. Sloan, Jr., 176

-N-

Napoleon, 211
Nassau, Bahamas, 63
National Battlefields Park, 136
Nations, independence of, 166
Nauvoo, Illinois, 228
Nazarene, humble, 23
Nebuchadnezzar, 81
Neighbor, 27, 198
  elderly, 204
Neighbors, 60, 61
Nelson, Lord, 144
Nelson's Monument, 144
Nelson, Thomas, Jr., 215fffff
New Orleans, battle of, 46
New Orleans, Louisiana, 148
New Jersey, 210
New Testament, 23, 55
New Year's Day, 27
New York, 214
New Zealand, 107, 221
Newsboy, 88
Newsman, American, 84
Newsman, 225
Newsmen, 106
Newspaper, 55, 103
Newspapers, 165
Newsweek, 162
Niece, 175
Night to Remember, A, by Walter Lord, ???
Nile River, 161
Nixon, Richard M., 154, 155, 156, 212ff
Nobleman 37
North Atlantic, 43
North America, 136
Nose, crooked, 45
Notebook, pocket, 59
Novels, historical, 115
Nutrition, 58

-O-

Oceans, 163
Office, 125, 203
  newspaper, 69
Officers, two British, 152
Offices, high government, 168
Oil, 189
Oil fields, Arabian, 105
Oklahoma, 97
Oklahoma, musical play, 35, 36
Old Testament, 181
Operations, mining, 93
Operator, lumber mill, 58
Optimism, 24

Optimist, Just an, 22ff
Optimists, 22
Orator, 185
Ore, samples of, 69
Orange County, Virginia, 74
Orange Free State, 93
Oratory, 52
Organ, 162
Organisms, animal, 121
Oswego, Fort, 138
Outlook, 86
Overseer, 88
Oysters, 120

-P-

Pacific, College of the, 125
Pacific Ocean, 54, 55
Paddle, wooden, 212
Padover, Saul K., 72, 73, 74
Palais, Montcalm, 136
Palm, 182
Palsy, man with, 33
  sevant with, 24
Paradise, 24
Parents, 184
Paris, France, 117, 209
Parliament, 164
Parliament, Houses of, 144
Parmelee, G. W., 138
Parra, Fernando Dimayuga, 180
Parrots, 180
Parties, painting, 222
Passion, 103
Paths, cleared from snow, 198
Patience, companion of good timing, 46
Patients, in hospitals, 44, 229
Patriarchs, forest, 20
Patrick, William C., 125
Paul, Apostle, 100, 106, 117, 186
Paul Revere and the World He Lived In,
  by E. Forbes, 151
Payne, Mr., 146
Peace, 154
Peace, Prince of, 90
Peacemakers, 37
Peaches, fresh, 107
Peale, Dr. Norman Vincent, 224ff
Peale, Ruth Stafford, 225, 226
Peanuts, 23
Pearl Harbor, 44
Pekin, Illinois, 113
Pekingese, 97
Peleliu, invasion of, 116
Pencil and scissors, read with, 58
Pencil, Power in a, 57ff
Pennsylvania, 125
People, Mexican, 180

People, older, 203
Persian Empire, 102
Peter, 24, 37, 186
Petty, Charles B., 76, 77
Philadelphia, 216
Phillips Petroleum Company, 78
Philistines, 141
Philosopher, 85
Phoenix, Arizona, 27
Physician, 115, 125
Physician, North Carolina, 209ff
Piano, 115
  grand, 223
Pig, Guinea,
Pineapple, 159
Pioneers, 43
Pioneers, Mormon, 56
Pipe, laying, 47
Pirates, 174
Pittsburg Pirates, 160
Planes, jet fighter, 125
Plantation, Virginia, 72
Plato, 122
Plays, of G. B. Shaw, 20
Poem, of Donna's, 28
Poet, 90
  narrative, 115
Poison, 122
Poland, 118
Pole, gaffing, 30
Police, Bahama, 64
  chief of, 60
Policeman, owed, 88
Polio, 34
"Pony Bob," 88
Pony Express, 88
Pool, mountain, 181
Porch, front, 120
Portals of the Past, 133
Potato, Idaho Russet, 189
Potato, volume, 22
Potatoes, producer of, 22
Pottage, 103
Praise, threat of, 224ff
Prayers, 187
Prayers, of little girl, 204
Pratt, Jerry, 29ff
Preparation, margin of, 185
Press Photographers of New York,
  annual exhibit, 191
Prime Minister, 165
Prince of Peace, 21, 32
Princeton, 72
Printer, 100
Prison, 106
Prison cell, 122
Prize, Pultizer, 100

Problems, 61
  or challenges, 191ff
  family, 223
Proctor & Gamble, 106
Professional, sport, 117
Progress, 126
Promotions, 131
Prophets, 21
"Prophets, Prince of," 90
Propulsion, jet, 125
Proverb, 131
Psychologists, 66
Purchase, Louisiana, 111
Purses, coconut palm, 63

-Q-

Quarter, French of New Orleans, 148
Quebec, Canada, 136, 137
Quietude, sylvan, 21

-R-

Rachel, 131
Rafts, little rubber, 54
Railroad, 210
Razor, 88
Reader's Digest, 196
Reason, let us together, 176ff
Receptionist, 180
Reck, Alfred Pierce, 106, 107
Recognition, 227
Record, water speed, 123
Redcoats, 153
Redeemer, 27
Redwood, 19ff
Redwoods, giant, 19ff
Refinery, oil, 78
Relations, family
Religion, 72
Reporter, 124, 162
Republic National Bank Building,
  188, 189
Research, motivational, 66
Residence, of Prime Minister, 165
Resolute, 155
Resurrection, 24
Revere, Paul, 151, 152, 153
Revolutionary War, 74, 215
Reward, 148
Rickenbacker, Captain Edward
  Vernon (Eddie), 54ff
Rides, car, 198
Rifle, Revolutionary War, 167
Rifleman, 124
Ritz-Carlton Hotel, 214
Robbers, 47
Robbery, simulated train, 69
Robin, young, 95

Rockies, 69
Rockwell, Norman, 89
Rodgers, Richard, 35
Romans, 96
Rome, 90
Roommates, 100
Romney, Ruth, 115
Roosevelt, Eleanor, 99
Roots, 182
Rules, governmental, 107
Russia, southern, 102

-S-

Sacrifice, to God, 77
Safari, 93
Safety, Committee of, 74
Sailboats, 120
Salmon, 127
"Salmon Capital of the World," 29
Salmon, king, 30
Samarkand, 102
I Samuel, 141
Samuel, Sigmund, 138
San Antonio, Texas, 190
San Blas, Mexico, 180
San Jacinto, 190
San Francisco, California, 133, 134, 135
Sand, 77
Sandburg, Carl, 185
Santa Anna, 189, 190
Santiago, Armando, 180
Saturday Evening Post, 89
Saul, King, 142, 143
Sawdust, 130
Scenery, Alpine, 194
Scholars, young, 99
School, grade, 174
  private, 216
Schweitzer, Albert, 99, 162
Science, 58
Scotland, 97
Scott, Sir Walter, 97, 114
Scripps-Howard Newspapers, 84
Sea, 30
Sears Roebuck & Company, 105
Sears, Robert N., 78
Seattle, Washington, 29
Security, 159
Sedan, four-door, 179
Seine River, 117
Self-importance, 71
Self-love, 71
Self-pride, 219
Self-respect, 71
Self-sufficient, 56
Seltzer, Louis B., 224
Seminar, 212

Senate, U. S., 33
Senator, U. S., 99
Serpents, 184
Servant, centurion, 37
Servants, 101
Service, hotel, 225
Setbacks, financial, 223
Seven Came Through, by Rickenbacker, 56
Seven Years War in Canada, The, by
    S. Samuel, 138
Seward, William H., 186
Shackelton, Sir Ernest H., 227
Shakes, redwood, 19
Shasta Dam, 159
Shaw, George Bernard, 20, 39, 228
Shaw, George Bernard, by G. K.
    Chesterton, 39
Sheep, 142
"Sheep, stray," 150
Sheepman, 222
Shepherds, 25
Shingles, cedar, 19
Ship, hospital, 116
Ships, cargo, 214
    merchant, 158
Shocks, 56
Shortcomings, 91
Sign, 23
Silas, 106
Silverton, Colorado, 69
Simplot, J. R., 22
Sinner, 37
Six Crises, by R. M. Nixon, 212
Skies, life's, 39
Skyline, Dallas, 188
Slag, dumping of, 120ff
Slaves, Israelite, 161
Sling, 143
Slivers, 19
Smelter, 120
Sloan, Alfred P., Jr., 167ff
Socrates, 121, 122
Sofa, 22
Sokoloniki, Oark, 154
Soldier, 168
Soldiers, 44
    American, 46
    British, 46
    Congolese, 84
Solomon, 61
Son, Prodigal, 155
Son, author's oldest, 87
    of Donna, 27
    of a drunken father, 207
    of a teacher, 178
    nine-year-old, 129
    six-year-old, 206

Sordello, 193
Soul, human, 214
Soup, Italian, 133
South America, 157
South Pole, 227
South Wales Medical Society, 53
Southey, Robert, 145
Soviet Russia, 154
Spain, 168
Speaker, 185
Spear, 142
"Spear, He Held His," 102ff
Spears, golden, 104
Speech, esophegeal, 192
Speedboat, 124
Spirit, poor in, 23
Spokane, Washington, 78
Sports, 58
Spots, on the rug, 131
Springfield, Massachusetts, 210
Springtime, 32
Spur, Give Yourself a, 99ff
St. George, Utah, 76
St. Matthew Passion, by Bock, 85
St, Lawrence River, 136
St. Petersburg, Russia, 210
Stagg, Amos, Alonzo, 125
Standard, basketball, 87
Standard Oil (New Jersey), 105
Statesmen, 112
Station wagon, 218
Statistics, 173
Statue, of a dog, 97
Stature, earthly, 21
Stebbins, Hal, 227
Stockton, California, 125
Stones, five smooth, 143
Stonington, Connecticut, 210
Store, general, 76
Stories, love, 131
Storm, on the sea, 32
Storms, 164
Stove, potbellied, 207
Strategist, 82
Strawberries, 204
Streams, 40
Streets, of Athens, 121
Streets, Two in One, 69ff
Strength, 117
Strengths, man's, 118
Students, interviewing top, 99
Submarines, enemy, 214
Success, 46, 76
Sugar, 63ff
Sunday School, 184
Sunday School class, 41
Suns, 39

Supper, last, 37
Surgery, 115
  heart, 95
  on nose, 45
Surveyor, frontier, 146
Susan, daughter, 30
Susquehanna University, 125
Sutter Street, 134
Sweat, 132
Sweaters, Tyrolean, 194
Synagogue, 23

-T-

Table, Captain's, 36
Talisman, The, by Sir Walter Scott, 115
Tall, they think, 188ff
Tamer, lion, 81
Tanks, 117
Tarbell, Ida M., 211
Tavern, 146
Taw, 60
Taylor, Henry J., 84
Taylor ,Henry Noble, 84
Teacher, able, 185
  college, 57
  stimulating, 178
Telegrapher, tramp, 58
Temper, 103
  spears of, 104
  violent, 146
Temptation, 158
"Ten Best Managed Companies, The,"
  105
Ten Commandments, 34
Tennessee, 189
Tensions, of the times, 33
Terhune, Albert Payson, 96
Termites, 180
Texas, 188, 189, 190
Thames River, 144
Thanksgiving, 215, 218ff
Theology, 58
Theatre, San Francisco, 192
"There'll Always Be An England,"
  music, 43
Thermopylae, heroes of, 190
Things, Tallest Living, 19ff
Thirkell, Angela, 156
Thomas, Dana Lee, 86
Thomas, Henry, 86
Thrust, 100
Ticonderoga, 138
Time, magazine, 23, 166, 212
Time, 82
  earthly, 21
Times, tempestuous, 213
Times, Los Angeles, 34

Times, New York, 98
Timing, 45ff
Timothy, 186
Titanic, ship, 43
Tithing, 225
Togetherness, Sweet, 42ff
Tokyo, Japan, 219
Tomatoes, 40
Tom Sawyer, The Adventures, of, by
  S. L. Clemens, 68
Tomorrow, timeless, 21
Town, Missouri farm, 67
  Welsh mining, 53
"Trafalgar, Battle of," 145
Trafalgar Square, 144, 147
Tragedy, 195
Trail, mountain, 206
Train, 219
  electric trolley, 194
  narrow gauge, 69
Travel, space, 100
Tree, Christmas, 127, 128, 129
Tree house, 93
Trenton, 168
Tribune, Oakland, 107
Tribune, The Salt Lake, 126
Tribesmen, 84, 94
Trip, Mexican, 181
  shopping, 127
  world-circling, 23
Trouble, 184
Tutor, 122
Twain, Mark, 68
Tyee, salmon, 30

-T-

Ullswater, 123
Ultimatums, 154ff
United States, 154
"Unknown God," 106
Ushio, Keinosuke, 220
U. S. News & World Report, 94

-V-

Vacation, 127
  family, 222
Vagrancy, 207
Vendrevil, governor of Canada, 137
Venezuela, 105
Venice, 193
Veterinary, 129
Victims, cancer, 192
Victoria, Queen, 229
Victory, 104
View, point of, 177
Violet, mountain, 40
Virgin River, 76

Virginia, 167, 216
Voice, 88

-W-

Waikiki Beach, 159
Wales, 163
Warden, prison, 60
Warner, Homer C. "Pug," 36
Warner & Swasey, 94
War of 1812, 145
Warship, British, 149
Warships, 91
Washington, D. C., 166
Washington, George, 74, 167, 215
Washington, George, Statue of, 144, 145
Wastebaskets, 89
  household, 87
Water, 130
  rough, 77
  shallow shoal, 163
Waters, Jesus walking on the, 32
Weddell Sea, 228
Welkom, Africa, 93
Western Hemisphere, 166
Westminster Kennel Club, 97
Westport, Washington, 29ff
Wheeler, Benjamin Ide, 103
"When Irish Eyes Are Smiling," music,
  44
Whistler, Anna McNeil, 209ff
Whistler, James, 210, 211
Whistler, George Washington, 209ff
White House, 166, 189
White, William Allen, 100
White, W. L., 56
Whitney, Tish, 196
Who's Who in America, 57
Widow, 91, 197
Widtsoe, John A., 36
Wildflowers, 206
William and Mary, 167
William Henry, Fort, 138
Williamsburg, 167
Wife, toiling, 119
Win, if we want to, 93ff
Windows, broken, 131
Wine, 82, 103
Wings, 130
Winter, 196
Wisdom, Secret of His, 60ff
Wisdom, Warrior's, 54ff
Wisdom, with kindness, 184
Wise men, 26
Wish, 90
Witherspoon, John, 73
Wolfe, James, 136
Woman, A Too, 26ff

Woman, 114, 115
  cleaning, 203
  colored, 63
  elderly, 218
  in sin, 37
  purchasing a blanket, 185
  Sunday School teacher, 40, 41
  undergoing heart surgery, 95
  who had sinned, 204
  with burdens, 44
  with cancer, 33
  young Texas, 188
Women, before Solomon, 61, 62
  sophisticated club, 228
Woods, 164
Words, Ten for Today, 32ff
Wordsworth, William, 39
Worker, construction, 115
Workman, Cornelius (Neil), 116
World, 86
  end of the, 114ff
World Book Encyclopedia, The, 101
World War I, 54, 117, 164, 165
World War II, 35, 40, 43, 53, 101, 105,
  116, 125, 158
Wounds, 176
Wright, Mary (Mrs. Cleo D.), 221ff
Wyoming, 116

-Y-

Yale, 125
Yorktown, 215
Young, Brigham, 161, 208
Youth, college, 214